Negotiating Skills for Managers

Other titles in the Briefcase Books series include:

To learn more about titles in the Briefcase Books series go to
www.briefcasebooks.com
You'll find the tables of contents, downloadable sample chapters, information on the authors, discussion guides for using these books in training programs, and more.

A
Briefcase
Book

Negotiating Skills for Managers

And Everyone Else

Steven P. Cohen

McGraw-Hill

New York Chicago San Francisco Lisbon London
Madrid Mexico City Milan New Delhi San Juan
Seoul Singapore Sydney Toronto

McGraw-Hill

A Division of The McGraw-Hill Companies

3 4 5 6 7 8 9 0   FGR/FGR   0 9 8 7 6 5 4 3

ISBN 0-07-138757-9

Library of Congress Cataloging-in-Publication Data applied for.

*This is a CWL Publishing Enterprises Book, developed and produced for
McGraw-Hill by CWL Publishing Enterprises, John A. Woods, President. For
more information, contact CWL Publishing Enterprises, 3010 Irvington Way,
Madison, WI 53713-3414, www.cwlpub.com. For McGraw-Hill, the sponsor-
ing editor is Catherine Dassopoulos, and the publisher is Jeffrey Krames.*

Printed and bound by Quebecor World Martinsburg.

McGraw-Hill books are available at special quantity discounts to use as pre-
miums and sales promotions, or for use in corporate training programs. For
more information, please write to the Director of Special Sales, McGraw-Hill,
2 Penn Plaza, New York, NY 10128. Or contact your local bookstore.

 This book is printed on recycled, acid-free paper containing a minimum of 50% recycled de-inked fiber.

Contents

Preface

When I told my father of my plans to develop a firm specializing in training people how to negotiate, he was quite surprised. When I indicated that many people feel the need to become more confident, he was dumbfounded. "Don't people know negotiating is fun?" he asked. But he's good at it and likes to make deals. The aim of this book is to help you get good at it as well and to increase your confidence and the resulting rewards that can come from concluding an effective negotiation.

The title of this book is *Negotiating Skills for Managers*, but a more descriptive title would include the subtitle "and Everyone Else." Negotiation is a universal human activity—we all engage in bargaining at one level or another on a pretty regular basis. And while we all need good negotiation skills in business, these skills are valuable in our personal lives as well.

Several years ago, in a response to a follow-up form asking for a long-term evaluation of our flagship negotiation course, a participant responded that he had not used negotiation in his professional life—but he had used it to save his marriage. I hope this book will enhance your professional skills as a negotiator; and then you can view any personal impact simply as an additional benefit.

Plan of the Book

Negotiating Skills For Managers has 12 chapters. In the first 10 we discuss negotiation paradigms, philosophical underpinnings, and specific tools and techniques. You'll find a detailed review of the idea of "interests" and BATNA (Best Alternative To a Negotiated Agreement)—two things all negotiators need to understand. There's also a discussion of the Interest Map©, a crucial preparation tool introduced in Chapter 5 and used in subsequent chapters. The two final chapters bring it all together, with Chapter 11 focusing on the negotiation process and Chapter 12 summarizing what I call the Seven Pillars Of Negotiational Wisdom©.

You'll find that *Negotiating Skills for Managers* does not promulgate a series of hard-and-fast rights and wrongs. Effective negotiators know that each negotiation has unique characteristics and being flexible can make the difference between effectiveness and wasted time. This book emphasizes that you should not view negotiation as a competitive exercise, and that the best way to conduct a successful negotiation is to aim for all parties to be satisfied when you conclude the agreement.

Special Features

The idea behind the books in the Briefcase Books series is to give you practical information written in a friendly person-to-person style. The chapters are short, deal with tactical issues, and include lots of examples. They also feature numerous boxed sidebars designed to give you different types of specific information. Here's a description of these sidebars and how they're used in this book.

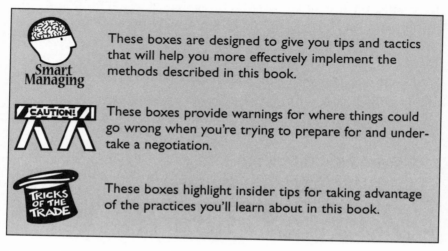

Smart Managing — These boxes are designed to give you tips and tactics that will help you more effectively implement the methods described in this book.

CAUTION! — These boxes provide warnings for where things could go wrong when you're trying to prepare for and undertake a negotiation.

TRICKS OF THE TRADE — These boxes highlight insider tips for taking advantage of the practices you'll learn about in this book.

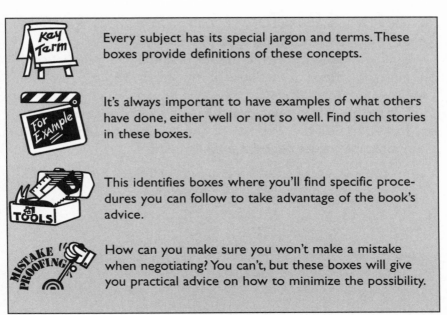

Every subject has its special jargon and terms. These boxes provide definitions of these concepts.

It's always important to have examples of what others have done, either well or not so well. Find such stories in these boxes.

This identifies boxes where you'll find specific procedures you can follow to take advantage of the book's advice.

How can you make sure you won't make a mistake when negotiating? You can't, but these boxes will give you practical advice on how to minimize the possibility.

Acknowledgments

While any mistakes in *Negotiating Skills for Managers* are my responsibility, I have been lucky enough to have received help and support from my wife, Andréa F. F. MacLeod, and my colleague Marsha M. Vaughan. John Woods, of CWL Publishing Enterprises, made the whole project possible, from his innovative formatting of the Briefcase Books series to his pointed editorial comments—and his effective prodding. Joan Paterson served as editor and had a lot to do with finalizing the manuscript that has become this book. In addition, Nancy Woods and Bob Magnan, also of CWL, had a hand in creating the final product you have before you.

This book also owes a considerable debt to ideas from colleagues within The Negotiation Skills Company, Inc.: Anthony Adamopoulos, Esq., Mary Ellen Shea, Ron Scruggs, Denise Delaney, Curtis Johnson, and Paul Cohen, Esq. Of the many others who have contributed to my understanding, Marshall Derby, Felicity Barber, Ricardo Altimira-Vega, and the late

Anthony Hyde stand out. My daughters Julia and Abigail have kept me on my negotiating toes all their life.

Fundamentally, however, my most significant negotiation learning took place at the knee of my father, Martin E. Cohen. I owe it all to him.

For further information and advice about negotiation, you are invited to visit the Web site of The Negotiation Skills Company, Inc.: **www.negotiationskills.com.**

About the Author

Steven P. Cohen is the founder and head of The Negotiation Skills Company, Inc., a consulting and training organization that has presented negotiation skills training to people from more than 40 countries. His clients come from business sectors as diverse as healthcare and the manufacture of nuclear weapons. The Negotiation Skills Company's mission statement is simple: to advance the cause of civility in negotiation to the benefit of all participants.

The breadth of Steve Cohen's experience, negotiating in the public and private sectors and working with people from all over the world, has given him a unique perspective on the do's and don'ts of negotiation. In *Negotiating Skills for Managers*, Steve offers his negotiation experience, communication skills, and teaching techniques to a broader audience.

His company's award-winning Web site, **www.negotiation-skills.com**, has subscribers from over 80 countries, on every continent except Antarctica. You can contact Steve at tnsc@negotiationskills.com.

Negotiating Skills for Managers

Competitive Versus Collaborative Decision Making

Negotiation is not a competitive sport.

Paul Murphy is on an extended business trip and getting pretty sick of staying in hotel rooms that all look alike even though they're in different cities. His company has a relationship with the hotel chain where he's been staying, but the business deal is for the least expensive room. How can he improve the accommodations when he checks into the next hotel?

Sally Marks manages a team in the design department of an automobile manufacturing company. A directive has arrived from the marketing department indicating the top priority for the next design cycle is to develop a vehicle that weighs no more than a ton, has space for five passengers, can cruise at 75 miles per hour for extended periods, complies with increasingly strict exhaust emission standards, and can fit into small urban parking spaces. The marketing department also wants manufacturing costs held substantially below any previous cars her group has designed—yet use high-tech materials.

Sally and her team's delivery on this combination of specifications will require the cooperation of members of teams from manufacturing, purchasing, and testing segments of the company. In addition, Sally has to cope with regulatory issues as well as external suppliers in order to accomplish her task.

When Fred and Jane Yancey and their two kids moved into their new home, it needed a lot of fixing up as well as an addition. Some of their neighbors have been very friendly—as well as understanding about the noise of construction machinery—but others have complained to the local building inspectors without talking first to Fred or Jane. The Yanceys are the first African-American family to move into the neighborhood. They wonder whether the complaints to the building inspector relate to the construction itself or whether other factors are involved.

As chief of her firm's team selling processors to a public sector utility company in China, Angela MacKenzie has to contend with competitors from the U.S. and other countries. But she is even more challenged by the process of figuring out how much progress she and her colleagues are making convincing the representatives of the Chinese utility company of the value of the processors they are selling.

Every day, all over the world, people find themselves in similar situations. They want to accomplish a particular task, clarify a relationship, or simply find resources to achieve more than they might by making a deal with someone else. They need to negotiate to get from their starting point to their objective.

Negotiating Skills for Managers is designed to help its readers understand and utilize a process that is fundamental to business—and the rest of life.

What Is Negotiation?

When people want to do something together—buy or sell an item, make a business deal, decide where to go for dinner—they need to use some sort of mechanism for reaching an

Waging Peace

In the old days, when wealthy landowners had a dispute they would hire mercenaries—knights—to wage war to determine who was right. The winner of the battle was acclaimed the winner of the dispute. Then somebody invented lawyers. For the past thousand years or so, we've been waging law to decide who wins. Today, as people rely increasingly on negotiation to resolve disputes or reach agreements, they are waging peace to reach the resolution that is most acceptable to all parties.

agreement. Unless they agree instantly on every element of the choices to be made, they need to use a mutually acceptable process for decision making. Negotiation is one name for a variety of joint decision-making processes, although people also use such terms as making a deal, trading, bargaining, dickering, or (in the case of price negotiation) haggling.

A successful negotiation has taken place when the parties end up mutually committed to fulfilling the agreement they have reached. Fairness is a crucial element to make a negotiation process succeed. Some people negotiate as if their most significant objective is to take advantage of other parties; this is self-defeating. If any party feels unfairly treated, he or she may walk away from the negotiation with a negative feeling and a disinclination to live up to the agreement.

One way to think of negotiation is to compare knitting and weaving. When you knit something, you generally use a single strand of yarn. And although knitted fabrics may contain a variety of colors and textures, you can easily stretch them out of shape. In weaving, the fabric is created by using at least two strands coming from different directions.

Negotiation The process of two or more parties working together to arrive at a mutually acceptable resolution of one or more issues, such as a commercial transaction, a contract, or a deal of any sort.

Negotiation is a give-and-take bargaining process that, when conducted well, leaves all parties feeling good about the result and committed to achieving it.

Woven fabrics tend to have greater tensile strength and durability than knitted fabrics. Negotiation is more like weaving—the process takes contributions from various parties. While weaving and knitting may involve a single person's skills, negotiation calls for contributions from two or more parties. By drawing upon the knowledge, skills, and other input of the multiple parties, a good negotiation process weaves together a durable agreement whose strength derives from the fact that the parties reached agreement by working together.

What Negotiation Is Not

When your boss gives you an order and your only choice is to do what he or she says, that is not negotiation. If an outsider is brought in to make a decision between parties using arbitration, the parties are legally bound to follow the arbitrator's decision. That is not negotiation. When parties are not working together to reach an agreement, negotiation does not take place.

It's important to keep in mind that negotiation is *not* a competitive sport. This doesn't mean, however, that we're never in a contest with other parties. But we are not competing with the aim of making sure we crush the opposition. Rather, we are aiming to do the best we can for ourselves. Using this philosophy, we are less interested in the sporting aim of competing and more interested in looking out for ourselves. In negotiation, you want to do well for yourself, but not because you want to beat someone else. Effective negotiation is held in its proper context as a mechanism for pursuing interests.

Your dealings with customers—or suppliers, neighbors, or relatives—should not be viewed as competitions. We negotiate with people to reach an agreement that meets as many of the parties' interests as possible. Our fundamental obligation is to pursue our own interests, assuming that the other parties are doing their best to get their interests met. We need to remember, however, that if the negotiating parties aren't satisfied with the process as well as with the result, odds are that the promises constituting the agreement won't be fulfilled. Negotiation based on individual interests requires that we open our minds and our strategizing to other parties' interests as well as our own. The definition of negotiation can now be expanded to describe how parties trade things of value in a civilized manner.

Types of Negotiation

People usually view negotiation as either confrontational or cooperative. People who view negotiation as a confrontation see the process as a zero-sum game in which a limited number of bargaining chips are to be won—and they want to be the winners. The confrontational winner-take-all approach reflects a misunderstanding of what negotiation is all about and is short-sighted. Once a confrontational negotiator wins, the other party is not likely to want to deal with that person again.

Cooperative-approach negotiators see a wide range of interests to be addressed and served. They understand that negotiation is not a zero-sum game but a way to create value for all the parties involved. The cooperative negotiator understands the importance of all stakeholders winning something—this is how you build long-term mutually beneficial relationships.

The cooperative approach is known as *interest-based negotiation*. Interest-based negotiation is particularly effective in a marketplace characterized by diversity. We often need to reach agreement with people who are different from us—culturally, ethnically, or economically. If we cannot get beyond the differences, they can create obstacles to agreement. To do this, we need to focus on the interests of the parties instead of on the parties' differences. Those interests can form the building blocks upon which agreement is based.

Key Term
Interest-based negotiation An approach to negotiation where the parties focus on their individual interests and the interests of the other parties to find a common ground for building a mutually acceptable agreement.

I'm Good, You're Good

Smart Managing When you brush your teeth in the morning, do you see a "good" or "bad" person in the mirror? Unless there's something extraordinary about you, you probably see a good person. It is important to remember that the other parties with whom you will be negotiating likely see "good" people in their mirrors as well. If all parties undertaking negotiation see themselves as good people, it makes sense for them to treat one another with that understanding. If you approach a deal-making process as an opportunity to crush the opposition, you are choosing to beat up on someone who views himself as a good person.

My Way or the Highway

Some people approach negotiation with an attitude that can be characterized as "my way or the highway." This occurs in a situation where one person believes that he or she holds all the cards in a negotiation. If you want something from that person, you may have to give him something he really values.

Think of your experiences in renting cars. Automobile rental companies have thought of all the answers; they ask you to sign and initial the front of the contract in several places. The actual contract is on the back of the paper you sign, generally printed in very small letters in extremely light ink. If you want a rental car, you can't negotiate the contract. The rental company has adopted a position from which they will not budge. There is no clearer example of the "my way or the highway" approach.

Key Term **Position** This is the final answer to the question "What do you want?" It can be okay to *start* with a position in a negotiation, but unless you understand the interests behind your position and are open to alternative approaches, you are likely to find yourself stuck in a corner you cannot escape without losing face.

Hazards of Adopting a Position

In negotiations between parties who each have some power to influence the results (the usual type of negotiation), the crucial thing to remember is that taking a position limits your capacity to bargain. A *position* is a party's answer to the question "What do you want?" If you adopt a position from which you will not budge, you run the risk of losing face if you have to back down from the approach you are using.

Investigating Your Interests

The more effective route to achieving an acceptable conclusion to a negotiation is to look at the interests of the parties. Your *interest* is the answer to the question, "Why do you want (a particular result)?" A problem arises when you ask the "why" question: Your response may be a justification of a party's *position* rather than an explanation of the *interest* that needs to be met. If the response to "Why do you want it?" is "Because it is in the company's best interest," your answer justifies a position but does not really explain the interests that underlie it. To move past justification to learn which interests are at the core of why someone wants something, you need to ask: How will that approach accomplish what you are looking for? or If we agree to do that, what goal of yours will it satisfy?

> ### Working with Deadlines
> Let's say you are told that a job has to be accomplished by a certain time. If you think the deadline threatens whether the job can be done as well as it should to yield the best results for your division, you need to go beyond the justification of the deadline of the person with whom you're negotiating and look at the interests the deadline is intended to serve.

Understanding Our Own Interests

One of the most difficult things to do is to understand our own interests. Since you and I tend to think that we are each a good person, it is easy to fall into the trap of thinking, "If I want it, it must be the best answer." However, you need to ask yourself—and

> **Positions and interests**
> Our *positions* can be thought of as what we want; our *interests* reflect what we need.

this can be tough—whether the way you want to do something is really the best approach, or whether taking another party's views into account might lead to even better results—or results that are better given that there are other people involved, not just yourself.

If we are making a retail purchase and have done a thorough job of research, we know which model of refrigerator or television we want to buy. That becomes our position. If one store doesn't have what we want, we look for a store that does, although this may be time consuming. If what you're looking for isn't readily available, the cost of the search may outweigh the benefits of sticking to your position.

In most negotiations, focusing on interests will make an enormous difference in the outcome. In buying the refrigerator, for example, your interests may include a certain size, color, and shelving flexibility. Through your research, you find one model that meets your criteria, but there may be others that meet your criteria equally well or even better. By looking at your interests— the benefits you expect to derive from achieving your negotiating goal—rather than at one specific outcome, and then keeping an open mind with regard to how you might take care of your interests, you're likely to discover there is more than one way to skin the proverbial cat. Let's explore this point further.

What Difference Does It Make to Distinguish Between Interests and Positions?

Distinguishing between interests and positions is a critical first step in understanding the negotiation process. If we can determine whether we and the other parties are undertaking interest-based negotiation or positional bargaining, we have a clearer idea of what is happening among us. When we use interests as the points from which we and the other parties are attempting to reach an agreement, everyone has greater flexibility in the decision-making process. This additional freedom provides the opportunity to think out of the box, to bring creativity to the process, and, as a consequence, to reach an agreement that will really work.

Using the interest-based approach rather than positional bargaining puts the negotiation process on a different footing. The fact is that most of the time we are negotiating with people we've negotiated with on previous occasions. Knowing that, the smart thing is to treat each negotiation as an episode in an ongoing relationship. Using the interest-based approach is the best way to make sure that happens. And if you're dealing with someone for the first time, the interest-based approach is the approach that will most likely help assure further deals in the future.

> ### Positions Limit Choices
>
> A position reduces the number of choices a party can make. If Charlie is unwilling to bargain or consider possible alternatives to the position Jackie has adopted, it reduces the choices available to Jackie. Taking a positional approach means you can't change your mind without risking losing credibility in the negotiation. That's why taking a position is usually not a good way to negotiate.

Besides exploring your interests, you need to prioritize them. For example, if you want to buy a car to commute to work, focusing on finding a model that will get good gas mileage and that will be easy to park may be a lot more important as an interest than whether the radio has four or six speakers. People who take the positional approach and make every element on their list of wants equally important will find it more difficult to find what they're looking for or to figure out on which things they might be able to compromise.

Focusing on interests also helps us overcome potential obstacles to agreement that arise from differences between people. Whether it is an Englishman negotiating with someone from Italy, a woman trying to sell an idea to a man, or a parent dealing

> ### Analyze the Process
>
> Understanding the negotiation process provides you with a critical tool. By giving you a "scientific" or analytical way of figuring out what's going on, it helps you avoid the pitfall of letting your emotions get in the way of your good sense as you engage in the negotiation.
>
> Smart Managing

with a child, cultural and experiential differences (along with individual preferences) can be challenging. Recognizing our own interests and, as much as we can, those of our negotiation counterpart, helps us navigate past potential obstacles to agreement.

How Do You Deal with Positional Bargainers?

Let's say you're dealing with a positional bargainer. What do you do? It's all well and good to approach joint decision-making efforts from an interest-based perspective. However, many people do not understand or do not accept the idea that while one-sided negotiations may yield short-term gains, they create the risk of long-term losses.

There are a variety of ways of dealing effectively with positional bargainers. Just as many Asian martial arts teach us to let others defeat themselves by allowing us to use their own strength to our advantage, in negotiation it is possible to respond effectively to heavy-handedness with a light touch. When people let off steam by shouting or using strong language, it is critical not to answer with the same sort of outburst. You can compare it to two waves heading toward each other: If they meet, the water becomes even more turbulent. If you think of yourself as able to control one of the waves by making it duck under the onrush of the other wave, the water smooths down after the wave has passed.

If you are negotiating with someone who comes up with an outrageous or unacceptable proposal, rather than trying to convince him by yelling even louder, it can be extremely effective to respond with silence. Sit there with a poker face and don't betray any emotion.

Let Them Vent!
Smart Managing When people get highly emotional—for example, when a young child throws a tantrum—the wisest thing to do is let the youngster ventilate his emotions without trying to control him. Once a person has spouted off, heart rate and breathing rate tend to slow down. The individual becomes calmer physically and generally more open psychologically to alternative ideas.

People tend to reflect a bit more when they're met with silence. They're likely to ask themselves, "What did I say? What did I do that offended him?"

Employees are often confronted with demands made by their boss. If you feel that the boss's idea is inappropriate in your situation, ask, "How do you think dealing with this situation in this way will impact our long-term relations with the client?"

Don't ask questions that allow for a yes or no answer—ask for explanations. If you've been told to sell a deal that you don't feel right about to a client or supplier, it's perfectly appropriate to tell your boss, "I want to do this job right. If you were me, how would you sell this approach to the other side?"

Fundamentally, when you're up against a positional bargainer who can't accept any alternatives to his or her ideas, rather than attacking the ideas—which may be taken as a personal attack—try to learn what interests underlie their position. By finding out what folks are really trying to achieve, you develop a better sense of how to present alternatives that will respond to their most important interests.

If you are in a salary negotiation, for example, learn how significant the various elements of a compensation package may be to an employer or an employee. If you ask questions about such issues as tax considerations, shares of equity ownership in the company, vacation time, flexible hours, indications of how important a particular outcome may be to a party's ego, or whether there are non-financial elements either party finds important, you may find one or more ways to break an apparent deadlock.

> **Dealing with Bullies**   Tricks of the Trade
>
> If you are negotiating with someone who is acting like a bully, keep in mind that bullies are afraid of failure. If you say, "I am afraid we may fail to reach agreement," there is a good chance that the threat of joint failure will act as a wake-up call to the bully, who may immediately change his or her behavior.

Is Money Really the Interest?

Often it seems that everything boils down to money. We place prices on things and on factors such as timely delivery or payment up front. It is important to recognize that just because money may appear to be the main interest of most or all of the stakeholders in a negotiation, don't assume that money means the same thing to each of them. As far as I know, there is only one person in the world to whom money has an intrinsic value—the Walt Disney character Uncle Scrooge. For most of us, money represents a means to fulfilling interests; for example, buying a new car, paying for your kids' college education, or as a measure of how much your employer values you. Money itself is not an interest; rather it is a means to an end, a mechanism for helping us achieve interests and measure value.

There's an old saying in negotiation: The first person to mention a dollar figure loses. If that were true, you and I could spend months going back and forth: "How much are you charging?" "I don't have a figure; what's in your budget?" "That depends on how much we have to spend." "Well, I need to know your price range so that I can offer you the right product."

In reality, we need to decide for ourselves ahead of time what price makes the most sense to us. If I'm negotiating my salary and my research of the market and my own needs indicate that I don't want

How Can We Recognize Interests?

Recognizing interests is one of the hardest parts of negotiation. Recognizing our own interests is not only challenging but also key to our capacity to negotiate intelligently. Ask yourself, "How many ways are there to achieve my objective and what desirable results do these alternatives have in common?" Finding common threads among desired results should help you understand more about your interests. Another approach is to ask, "What would be the negative consequences to me if my goal is not achieved?" When you find those negatives, turn them around into the missing positive consequences to get a clearer picture of the interests you're pursuing.

less than $50,000, a wise response to the query, "How much are you looking for?" is "I'm thinking in the range of the low 50s." This tells the boss that I'm looking for something between $50 and $55 thousand dollars. My boss may feel good offering $51,000, figuring she's saved $4,000 on the payroll budget. Or she may respond by saying, "I'm thinking more of a figure in the low 40s." Either way, it gives us a range within which to negotiate a figure we hope will lead to a mutually agreeable result.

Primary (Fundamental) and Secondary (Derivative) Interests

Let's say I want a new car. There are lots of reasons for choosing cars: getting more reliable transportation than my old car, impressing my peers (or members of the opposite sex), coping with the commute to a new job location, or celebrating a major accomplishment. Some of those reasons relate to solving practical problems—reliable transportation or commuting. Others relate to my ego—making an impression or celebrating an accomplishment.

If my most significant interests relate to transportation, my car search may lead in the direction of safety, gas mileage, or other practical considerations. If my ego interests are at the forefront, then perhaps I'll be more concerned with the brand name, model, or how well equipped the car is.

Fundamental or primary interests For any person engaged in a negotiation, these are results that go to the heart of your needs. Where the results that serve your interests come from is not important; it is the centrality of their importance to you that makes interests primary.

Derivative or secondary interests These interests need to be met before it is possible to address and satisfy your primary interests. If your primary interest is to live a comfortable old age, a derivative interest could be to make enough money to provide for that comfort. Another derivative interest that could precede comfort in your old age is preserving your health as best you can.

Rarely does a negotiation decision revolve around a single interest. Generally, there are *fundamental* or *primary* interests and *derivative* or *secondary* interests. Sometimes, in order to satisfy a fundamental interest, the first thing we need to do is deal with another derivative interest without which we cannot satisfy the big one. If I am buying a car for ego purposes, I may have an interest in amassing sufficient funds and paying off existing debts in order to be able to increase my capacity to buy a fancier car. Yet the same holds true if safe reliable transportation is the underlying interest. The more money I have available, the greater the likelihood I can afford a car with more safety features or a better warranty.

It is interesting, in the example of a car purchase, to see that while the fundamental interests—transportation or ego—may be different from each other, the derivative interest may be the same. Improving your financial situation in order to afford a car that serves your transportation or ego interests is important in either situation. Your interest in pursuing strategies relating to money may well lead you to undertake negotiations that have nothing to do with buying a car; but unless you exert your efforts in the direction of improving your financial status, you are less able to undertake the negotiations with car dealers to pursue your underlying primary interest.

This relatively simple situation gives us a sense of how important it can be to prioritize interests to develop a reasonably clear sense of what must be done to take us to the next step. Let's say that impressing your colleagues with a fancy car will meet the fundamental interest of boosting your self-image. In that case, buying the right car is a derivative interest designed to help fulfill the fundamental interest. However, to fulfill the derivative interest of getting the right car, you have to improve your financial picture—yet another derivative interest. And if one of the ways to get into better financial shape is to get a raise at work, there's yet another interest on your list. In order to get a raise, do you have interests in getting a promotion, being rewarded with a bonus for a particular achievement, or

gaining recognition from your longevity on the job? It is important to recognize that we often have to negotiate different things
with different parties to satisfy secondary interests before we are
in a situation where we can undertake negotiations focused
more directly on our primary interests.

As you can see, while we have certain fundamental interests
that underlie our negotiation activities, we may have to strate-
gize as if we're playing a game of billiards—thinking several
moves ahead and not just the immediate need to hit the 3-ball
into the side pocket. When we comprehend the relative priority
of our interests, it helps us develop longer-term strategies that
increase the likelihood that our fundamental interests will be
addressed. We need to understand what steps to take—and in
what order—to reach our interests. Look behind each of your
interests and figure out whether it is a fundamental/primary
interest or a derivative/secondary interest that needs to be met
before you can pursue the primary one.

Looking Beyond Our Personal Interests

When we negotiate, we need to consider our own interests first.
Focusing on our own interests helps protect us from developing
a competitive mentality where we might sacrifice important
interests in order to beat the "opposition." If we allow ourselves
to get carried away with beating the other guy, we may lose
sight of our interests and make decisions that go against those
interests. However, our interests are not the only ones at play in

Constituents Parties whose interests are affected by our
actions, particularly those who are depending on us to deliver. For example, these can include the boss, other colleagues
at work, or end-user customers.

Approach Another term for a substantive element of a negotiation.
My approach may be to sell the real estate to raise funds for the company. Your approach may be to sell off a division to raise those funds.
In each case, we need to look at which approach offers more promise
in light of the interests involved.

negotiation. We must give thought to the interests of our constituents: the company, our family, or members of our team at
work. Which interests of those constituencies are primary and
which are secondary? How do those interests influence the
approach we take in a given negotiation?

If we make a promise that creates a hardship for our colleagues—for example, promising delivery far faster than is realistic—we can get into trouble. While this does not mean we should
be paranoid negotiators looking over our shoulder all the time,
knowing that other groups have a stake in the outcome of our
negotiation helps put things in context, gives us a broader perspective, and increases the likelihood that we'll reach an agreement that comports well with the interests of our constituents.

In addition to looking at our constituents' interests, we need
to pay careful attention to the interests of parties with whom we
are negotiating. Learning what their interests are can help us
craft a solution that makes for a successful negotiation. Let's
look at the automobile purchase example. If we know we are
selling to someone to whom ego issues are more significant
than transportation, that helps us understand what perspective
will help them make their decision. The knowledge will help us
do a better job and, more than likely, make a better deal. Our
sales pitch in those circumstances should focus on things like
power, appearance, or the characteristics of people

Listen to Their Answers to Your Questions
Understanding our own interests may well be something we
can do by ourselves. Getting a handle on the interests of our
constituents, our negotiating partner, and our partner's constituencies
requires serious information gathering. We must ask questions to learn
about other parties' interests. More important, when we ask questions
we have to *listen* to the answers. To use an analogy, when someone
hands you their business card, it is considered good manners to read
each line of it before you slip it into your pocket. It shows that you
are paying attention and taking the person seriously. The same is true
in asking questions in negotiation; if your mind appears to wander as
folks give you answers, you send a negative signal.

buying the fancy cars we offer. If transportation is the issue, we are more likely to bring about a sale by focusing on fuel economy, our service department, and safety features.

Similarly, we must do our best to learn about the interests of our negotiating partner's constituencies. Those interests may drive his decision, and the more we comprehend his constituents' interests in our strategy and tactics, the greater the likelihood that the agreement we reach will provide our negotiation partner something to bring back to whomever he considers the powers that be.

The Three C's of Interests*

People often fool themselves into thinking that the objective of interest-based negotiation is to reach agreement on *common* interests. Common interests can be described as interests in which each party has the same reasons for wanting the same results. While it is certainly possible to find common interests through the negotiation process, more often than not we and our negotiation partners reach agreement because the interests met by the solution that is achieved are *complementary*.

Complementary interests can work in tandem. You have your interests, I

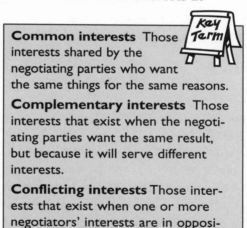

Common interests Those interests shared by the negotiating parties who want the same things for the same reasons.

Complementary interests Those interests that exist when the negotiating parties want the same result, but because it will serve different interests.

Conflicting interests Those interests that exist when one or more negotiators' interests are in opposition to interests of other negotiators.

have mine, but we can pursue each party's interests by undertaking a single action or a group of related actions.

Compromise: Where Does It Fit?

Notice that *compromise* is not listed among the Three C's of interests. Compromise is a mechanism for meeting in the middle,

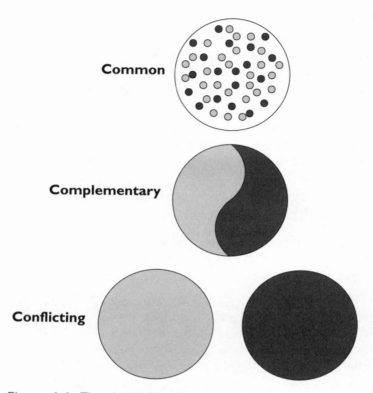

Common

Complementary

Conflicting

Figure 1-1. The three C's of interests illustrated©

requiring each party to give up an equivalent portion of their
objectives in order to arrive at an agreement. Compromise tends
to be most effective when the currency of the bargaining is limited. The currency of the bargaining is the range of assets that may
be traded among the negotiating parties. Thus, when money
alone is the issue that divides the parties—say I am asking you
for $20 and you are offer-
ing to pay $10 for an
item—splitting the difference and settling on a
price of $15 requires each
of us to give up the same
amount ($5).

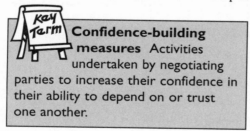

**Confidence-building
measures** Activities
undertaken by negotiating
parties to increase their confidence in
their ability to depend on or trust
one another.

Complementary Interests

One of the classic examples used in negotiation books and training courses to illustrate how finding complementary interests can lead to a mutually agreeable solution is often referred to as the Orange Story. Two folks are dickering over which of them gets one or more oranges—depending on the story. In each version, one of the people wants the orange juice and the other wants the orange rind. Sometimes the juice and rind are both to be used in eating or cooking; sometimes the two parts of the orange are needed to produce chemical or biological products that are highly valuable. The bottom line of each version of the Orange Story is that the parties have complementary interests: If I get the juice and you get the rind, we can share the orange rather than fight over who wins.

Sometimes we discover the parties' interests are in *conflict*. They have nothing in common, and there do not appear to be complementary interests that will make it easy to reach an agreement.

When it appears that interests are in conflict, negotiators have to weigh their options and determine whether it's in their interest to undertake or continue negotiations with a specific other party or whether it is better to look for another solution. Often there is no realistic alternative; the problem needs to be addressed by parties who, on the surface and perhaps even deeper, have conflicting interests as they relate to the problem at hand. Utilizing confidence-building measures (defined in detail later), reducing the issues under consideration to small building blocks, or using questioning and listening techniques to build a relationship can help reduce the challenges conflicts create.

When Interests Conflict

If you have no choice but to try to reach agreement with a party whose interests conflict with yours, build the possibility of agreement from the ground up. Look for small things about which you can agree—the time and place you'll meet, what items belong on the agenda and the order in which they should be discussed, the interests you and the others may share in an irrelevant topic such as sports, politics, or food. For example, perhaps a first—or early—meeting should take place at an ethnic restaurant where it is normal for diners to order and share entrees.

Make a serious effort to examine the issues that need to be resolved and look for small elements about which you and your negotiation partner don't disagree. It can be helpful to spend time agreeing on language that describes the problem, on possible resolutions that you both agree make no sense, or on short-term fixes to minor elements of the problem that each party finds acceptable. In international diplomacy, these approaches are often called confidence-building measures. The parties to a conflict need to develop confidence in each other before they can work together in a collaborative, cooperative way to reach an agreement. The parties' confidence in one another can be increased as they reach agreements on logistical matters such as the date and time of the negotiation, elements to be included in the agenda, or the shape of the bargaining table.

Reducing the substance of the problem to small units or utilizing confidence-building measures may fail to bring about a quick resolution, particularly to a long-standing conflict. However, such efforts can lay the groundwork for a reduction in the emotional level of the conflict and help the negotiating parties develop a civilized way for communicating with each other. The problem most likely will not simply go away without further effort. In the *Tao Te Ching*, Lao Tzu tells us, "The journey of 1000 miles begins with the first step." This is a useful observation and can help us on the route to reducing the barrier of conflicting interests that may make reaching agreement appear impossible. For unless we start, we cannot finish.

Manager's Checklist for Chapter 1

❑ A negotiation is only successful when it yields true buy-in from the parties. Successful negotiations yield mutual agreement in which each party is committed to fulfilling his or her promises.

❏ Negotiation is like weaving. By drawing upon contributions from more than one source of ideas or assets, it yields a fabric that has greater durability than an agreement that has only drawn its ideas from one side.

❏ Positional bargaining, the "my way or the highway" approach, locks a negotiator into a situation in which he will risk losing face if he backs down from what he has stated he wants.

❏ Interest-based negotiation focuses on the underlying reasons behind each negotiator's objectives. Opening yourself to considering how other parties' ideas may serve your interests as well as—or better than—your initial idea increases the likelihood you will gain from the process.

❏ Focusing on interests can help negotiators overcome or get around obstacles presented by cultural differences.

❏ Understanding and focusing on your own interests can help you overcome the instinct to treat negotiation as a competition between the parties.

❏ In analyzing your interests, as well as the interests of others, figure out which interests are primary and which take a secondary role. Sometimes you have to address secondary interests before it is possible to deal effectively with primary interests. Understanding this helps develop an effective negotiation strategy.

❏ Negotiation can include multiple stakeholders, not just the face-to-face negotiators.

❏ While money often seems to be the most common interest among the negotiators, remember that it means different things to different people. It can help achieve very different interests—and sometimes those interests are even better served when something other than money is the solution about which the parties agree.

❏ Remember the Three C's of interests: Common, Complementary, and interests that are in Conflict. Most successful negotiations end up with solutions that serve Complementary interests.

❏ When conflict exists, it often takes confidence-building measures to increase the capacity of the parties to negotiate with one another.

BATNA—Choosing Whether to Walk Away

You've got to know when to hold 'em,
And know when to fold 'em.
Know when to walk away,
And know when to run.
                    —From "The Gambler"*

Making Choices

Negotiations are about making choices. First we need to decide whether negotiating is the best way to resolve the issue we're facing. Then we have to determine with whom we're going to negotiate. And then we have to assess whether we are better off leaving an unpromising negotiation. These sorts of decisions depend on our assessment of our BATNA, our Best Alternative To a Negotiated Agreement.

In all negotiations, each party has a BATNA. Our walking-in BATNA consists of the elements of a solution over which we have a measure of control. We may be able to accomplish our

BATNA A party's BATNA is their Best Alternative To a Negotiated Agreement. Your BATNA is not your bottom line. It is a measure of the balance of power among the negotiating parties based on the resources they control or can influence to respond to their interests that will be addressed in a given negotiation. As described below, understanding the difference between "walking-in" BATNA, that group of resources in your pocket before negotiation begins, and the dynamic BATNA that changes as you gain information during the negotiation process gives you a sense of whether to undertake a negotiation and whether to quit once the process has begun.

objectives without outside help, we may have a choice among several competitors, or we may know that the other parties with whom we are to negotiate cannot achieve their objectives without our cooperation. Before the negotiation begins, we already have a known situation. Therefore, we should walk in to the negotiation process understanding our capacity to resolve issues on our own or with the help of a number of other parties.

Balance of Power

BATNAs are a measure of the balance of power among parties. If I need your help more than you need mine, you have a stronger BATNA and the balance of power to influence the outcome of the

CAUTION!

Strengthening and Weakening BATNAs

Strengthening your BATNA or weakening the BATNA of other parties aims at improving the likelihood of meeting your interests. Be careful not to work against the interests of other parties. This will reduce their incentive to deal with you, as it could reduce their opportunity to gain from the negotiations.

negotiation favors you. Developing a sense of the relative strength of the BATNAs of the negotiating parties is an important goal of the preparation process. Think about how to strengthen your walking-in BATNA as well as how to weaken the walking-in BATNA of the parties with whom you are negotiating.

Keep in mind that the balance of power—the relative strength of each party's BATNA—does not guarantee the outcome of the negotiation. Other factors such as the depth of your interest in reaching agreement with a specific party, the desirability of the BATNA available to you, or your concern about a long-term relationship can influence the outcome of an attempt to solve the problem when the balance of power is not equal. Examining choices—such as who you can choose as a negotiation counterpart, which of your interests takes priority, or what kind of information you require—both prior to and during the negotiation process can help you overcome an unfavorable power balance.

Understanding Our BATNA Offers Choices

Understanding our BATNA helps us decide when it makes more sense to walk out of a negotiation than to continue. Before we undertake negotiations, it is important to be aware of statements other parties might make indicating that continuing the

Sometimes Desperation Helps

On a flight from New Orleans to Dallas/Fort Worth, I was in a window seat on a crowded airliner. Even before my seatmates arrived, I was feeling claustrophobic. When the woman in the middle seat sat down, my claustrophobia level increased considerably. Then her husband arrived, obviously recently released from the hospital and in such discomfort that he could not bend enough to fit into the coach-class seat. When a flight attendant attempted to help by pushing him down into his seat, he screamed in pain. My feelings of claustrophobia were beginning to set an all-time record for intensity.

I wanted things to change, but my BATNA was weak compared with that of the flight attendant. In desperation, I yelled to the flight attendant, "This man is in pain! He should be given a seat in first class!" Somehow that made sense to her, and she found him a seat in the front of the plane. The woman next to me moved over to the aisle seat, giving me space to breathe. My claustrophobia subsided. Despite my weak BATNA, my interest in avoiding a claustrophobic panic attack helped me take the step needed to solve my problem.

Know When to Fold

Many years ago I was a lobbyist for the city of Boston in Washington. Soon afterward, Massachusetts became the only state to vote against the re-election of Richard Nixon. Then I visited a friend in the White House in hopes of gaining federal funds to aid Boston's celebration of the American Bicentennial. I was introduced to the White House's Bicentennial Coordinator, who asked if I would like to hear the White House's view of the Bicentennial. "I'm all ears," I replied. "We at the White House view the Bicentennial as an opportunity to celebrate the contributions Richard Nixon has made to American History," she declared. With that statement, my BATNA became crystal clear; I had nothing to gain from pursuing negotiation with this person. Her stated interest in focusing on President Nixon could not be addressed in the only state that had opposed his re-election. My BATNA was to take a walk from the situation.

Interestingly, I had thought that my walking-in BATNA was strong. Boston had played a significant role in the American Revolution and an excellent present-day staff had created truly imaginative plans for the Bicentennial celebration. How could the White House Bicentennial Coordinator do anything but thank me for bringing in our ideas and then send me, with her blessing, to the appropriate funding sources? How indeed! The information she gave me totally changed my BATNA.

discussion does not make sense. If you and I are on completely different wavelengths, it may well be that neither of us has what it takes to help solve the other's problem. This does not necessarily mean an extreme situation of conflict. On a simpler level, if you are looking for a house with three bedrooms and the house I am selling has only two, however much we may enjoy talking with each other, it clearly doesn't make sense to carry forward our negotiations about the house.

If we understand our BATNA, we know the range of resources available to deal with the problem we want to resolve. The problem is not just a matter of disagreement; it can also include the desire to buy needed raw materials or to find funding for a project.

What Is Our Walking-in BATNA?

When we want to accomplish a particular set of objectives, we need to assess the resources we require to reach our goals.

- Are the resources people or things over which we have control or influence?
- Do we have an ongoing relationship with a company that can help fulfill those needs?
- Are there many competitors looking for the opportunity to do business with us?
- Do we face serious competition?
- Are we up against a deadline?

Answers to each of these questions helps us understand our BATNA, the extent of power with which we walk into negotiations. The more we can help ourselves and the less we need others, the stronger is our walking-in BATNA.

If you feel your walking-in BATNA is weak, take a look at the resources available to you. What do you control? What can you influence in order to strengthen your BATNA? For example, say you manage a small company where some folks have sales as part of their job. Are you better off finding a hired-gun star salesperson from outside on a short-term contract, or would it be better to encourage relevant members of the staff to take an outstanding training program so that their enhanced skills stay within the company for the long term? This is one approach to analyzing your walking-in BATNA and finding a way to strengthen it inhouse.

Does BATNA Ever Change?

The quotation at the beginning of this chapter is from a song describing a seasoned poker player giving advice to a card player with less experience. It can be helpful to compare negotiation to playing cards. Every time a new card is dealt to you, it changes your BATNA or, in a card game, your sense of whether you have a good or not-so-good chance with a particular hand of cards. In many card games, the cards are dealt in such a way that only the recipient of those cards knows what they are. The player may be able to develop confidence in the power of his or her hand, but won't know anything about the relative strength of the cards in other players' hands. By contrast, in many card games some of the cards are dealt face up so that you can see some of the other players' cards—and they can see yours. In that situation, you can see elements of the BATNAs of all the players changing as the game goes forward.

Information

Information is the fundamental asset in negotiation. When you're negotiating a purchase, you need information on price, delivery, and specifications. This sort of information is what is communicated between negotiating parties. Even if you are familiar with the market, there may be details that make one supplier's products, or deal, more likely to satisfy your interests. As these details can change fairly quickly, pursuing information to do reality checks can serve your interests significantly.

When we negotiate, we are looking for information about our own BATNA and the BATNA of other negotiating parties. The better we understand the other parties' BATNAs, the greater the likelihood we'll reach a wise agreement. Understanding whether another party is bluffing is a critical element. We need to ask probing questions in order to gain information that can provide meaningful clues on how to go forward with the negotiation.

The Dynamic BATNA

Every time we gain information during the negotiation process, our BATNA changes. This dynamic quality of our BATNA is critical to understand. Keeping track of our BATNA while we negotiate is crucial to knowing whether we are wasting our time or whether continuing negotiation is a good idea. Moreover, our negotiation preparation process should include attention to factors that may arise during the actual negotiation that could change our BATNA.

There's an old rule in sales: When folks start agreeing with you, it's time to stop talking. In preparing for negotiation, you need to arrive at a guesstimate as to which factors will be most convincing to others with whom you are trying to reach agreement. Your understanding of your

> **Negotiation partner** The people or organizations with whom we negotiate can be referred to in many ways: partners, counterparts, or parties. We are not negotiating with opponents; they are the people with whom we compete. We negotiate with our negotiation partners in order to collaborate to reach an agreement that each of us will willingly fulfill.

BATNA may include a sense of what you need to reveal and which factors may not be of interest to your negotiation partner. As the exchange of information goes forward, you may learn that points you at first thought were an important part of your BATNA—or theirs—are simply not that important or convincing. Your BATNA changes and you have to deal with that change in pursuit of a better result.

BATNA Is Not the Bottom Line

It can be easy to jump to the conclusion that our bottom line objective is also our BATNA. This mistake can close our mind to the variety of possible ways we can reach a resolution with other parties that may not have occurred to us when thinking on our own.

Let's say your boss tells you to achieve a specific sales objective. If you analyze the alternatives, both in terms of potential customers and structuring of deals, the sales objective may be a bottom line. The variety of ways to achieve the bottom line, however, constitute the elements of your BATNA.

Sometimes a negotiating party is so positional, insisting on his way or nothing, that you may confuse the inflexibility of that stance with his BATNA. The party may be focusing on his bottom line and ignoring the choices available to reach an agreement that makes sense to both of the negotiating parties.

Bottom line focus reduces your flexibility. It can also force you to show your hand before it makes sense to do so. Giving your negotiating partner the opportunity to learn that you have choices, that you do have a decent or even a particularly strong BATNA, may increase your capacity to bargain without giving away the store.

Elements of BATNAs

BATNA is a complex mixture of factors that can influence the development and implementation of your negotiation strategy, your use of tactics during the process, and your conclusion about whether continuing negotiation is the best way to pursue your interests. Because of BATNA's dynamic nature, you need to keep an idea of how each piece of information exchanged during negotiation changes the BATNAs of the negotiating parties.

Deadlines

If you are under pressure to deliver a particular result within a tight time frame, your BATNA may be weaker than the BATNA of a party who at least claims to have all the time in the world. When people with whom you are negotiating know you have to make a decision in, say, three days, they have an incentive to keep you talking so that you don't have a chance to investigate alternatives offered by their competitors. Moreover, when folks know you're up against a tight deadline, they may negotiate more positionally, figuring that you won't have time to get them to improve the terms they're offering.

You have to consider whether revealing your deadline advances your interest or strengthens your BATNA in a negotiation. If you are a buyer, the deadline you face may offer a means of putting pressure on sellers to stretch to offer a more attractive deal. There is no hard-and-fast rule about revealing your deadline. You need to be aware and analytical in each case, deciding whether it is in your interest to let others know your time constraints.

Other parties' deadlines are an element of their BATNA. In

effect, the situation is a mirror image of what you face in terms of revealing or concealing your own deadlines. If you really need to know what kind of deadline your negotiation partner faces, you can always ask direct questions or a more subtle variation: "When have you promised to deliver the finished product (which includes our component) to the ultimate consumer?"

Alternatives

Remember the definition of BATNA: Best *Alternative* To a Negotiated Agreement. In each negotiation, you need to measure how each choice you make can influence the likelihood that the negotiation will yield favorable results. Be on the lookout for signals that you've gone as far as you can and that you should quit while you're ahead—or before matters get worse.

Your Own Resources

As you review your BATNA, it is crucial to take a long hard look at the resources you can influence or control to resolve the problem or achieve the objective.

> **Assessing Our BATNA**
>
> In assessing our BATNA we may face a variety of alternative ways to resolve our concerns or meet our objectives:
> • Several companies may be competing for our business.
> • We may prefer to deal with some people and not others.
> • Some potential negotiation partners are stuck with a commitment to conform to standard operating procedure while others respond with creativity and out-of-the-box thinking.

- Are there personnel within your organization who have the skills and the time and are available to provide the assistance you need?
- Do you have good relationships with the personnel with those capacities?
- Do you or does someone you can rely on have the capability to think out of the box to get the job done?
- At what point do you conclude that negotiation with

someone from another "tribe" within your company is the best way to meet your goals?

Part of determining how the available resources contribute to your BATNA requires understanding whether there is more than one way to meet your interests. Taking a positional approach, "This is the only way it can be done," weakens your BATNA as it limits the choices you can make.

Other Parties' Resources

Just as understanding the resources you can bring to bear in order to resolve an issue, you need to understand what resources other parties can bring to the table. If the resources they offer to solve the problem are more comprehensive or more useful than yours, clearly that means that their BATNA is stronger—at least in that area. The risk is that many people often forget that everyone puts their trousers on one leg at a time. Be careful not to assume that just because the people you're negotiating with come from another organization or are a different element of your own company, they must have more resources. Ask questions before and during negotiation to ascertain what resources they can control or influence; then your picture of the relative strength of the parties' BATNA will be more accurate.

Information

The more information we have about the subject matter of the negotiation, the greater our capacity to assess our BATNA and the BATNA of parties with whom we're negotiating. If we are knowledgeable about the product or service that's under discussion, that's good. If we are more knowledgeable than other parties, that's even better. We do have to be careful not to assume we know more than other people, however. Using the negotiation process to do a reality check on the accuracy of our assumptions is critical. Often people with many years of experience in a particular field assume that they have more knowledge than a younger, less-experienced person. If this viewpoint leads to laziness and a failure to prepare, the BATNA of the more experienced party is weakened. You can pull wool over the *eyes* of person, but I don't think you can pull wool over the *ideas* of someone who's newer at the game. In fact, it can be an unpleasant surprise to find that the "newbie" knows as much as or more than he does.

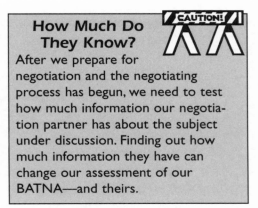

How Much Do They Know?

After we prepare for negotiation and the negotiating process has begun, we need to test how much information our negotiation partner has about the subject under discussion. Finding out how much information they have can change our assessment of our BATNA—and theirs.

Experience

Experience informs us about the subject matter of each negotiation. In addition, our experience working with other parties gives us a sense of their level of sophistication, their capacity to make and fulfill agreements, and their negotiation style. If we know someone reasonably well, we can draw on our own experience to assess those elements of our BATNA that may be based on past history or known characteristics of the people and/or the organization they represent.

If we lack experience working with the people or organization with which we'll be negotiating, the wisest move is to confer with colleagues or others who can advise us on what to expect. Having the benefit of a colleague's experience can help us in our assessment of our walking-in BATNA. Our colleague

What Does Our Experience Tell Us? Smart Managing

It is important to keep in mind that, in negotiation, the past has no future. Negotiating about the past is like two divorcing spouses who spend all their time fighting over which of them deserves more blame. The only way to survive a divorce or a business relationship with a stormy history is to focus on "How we want things to be in the future." We can change the future; all we can change about the past is our interpretation of it.

may tell us that the parties with whom we negotiate may have changed since the last time they negotiated with the company. Or perhaps we will learn that the other negotiators may take a different attitude because of changed business conditions or a different feeling about our personality as compared to our company's previous negotiator. If we're relying on that set of assumptions, the number one job is to do a quick reality check to see whether our colleague's experience can be relied upon during our own negotiation process.

Interests

A clear understanding of our interests, the priority or significance of each interest, and knowing how possible solutions can help achieve those interests give us additional comprehension of our BATNA. Certainly the same is true as we look at other parties' BATNAs. Knowing what our interests really are can help us have a better sense of whether we can meet them with our own resources or with the parties with whom we should negotiate and what benchmarks we can use to determine whether the negotiation offers a promise of yielding worthwhile results.

Keep Your Eyes on the Prize
Remembering that negotiation is not a competitive sport reminds us to keep our eyes on whether a given negotiation is bringing us closer to achieving our objectives and meeting our interests. It is easy to get led astray by emotion or issues that are really red herrings. Keeping our interests in mind is the best way to benchmark the process of a negotiation and to determine whether it is worth continuing or heading in a different direction.

Knowledge

The more we know about the subject matter of the negotiation, the characteristics of parties with whom we'll be negotiating, our capacity to deliver with the acquiescence of our colleagues, the stronger our BATNA in terms of our competence. Moreover, the more competent we feel about negotiating on a particular subject, the more confident we feel. Some people might question

Don't Confuse Confidence and Arrogance

A negotiator who exudes confidence because she is knowledgeable about the subject matter, understands the negotiation process, and is clear on her objectives is likely to be taken seriously by other negotiating parties. On the other hand, someone who swaggers into a negotiation with an attitude of arrogance is likely to be viewed as offensive. Arrogant negotiators with strong BATNAs can generate a personal dislike that may increase the other parties' motivation to negotiate more aggressively in order to teach the arrogant negotiator a lesson.

whether confidence itself is a measurable element of their BATNA. If you examine your negotiation experience, however, you will probably recognize that whenever you have run across negotiators who exude confidence, the balance of power is tipped further in their direction.

Strengthening and Weakening BATNAs

If BATNAs are units for measuring the balance of power, we have to be cautious about getting caught in the trap of thinking that (a) the balance is set in stone or (b) the party with a stronger BATNA always wins.

Creativity, greater commitment to a particular outcome, or focusing on other parties' interests may well overcome their apparent BATNA power advantage. Nonetheless, it is important to act in advance of negotiations to strengthen our own BATNA and weaken theirs.

If several different parties are involved in making a decision, parties that don't participate in the negotiation process are far less likely to have their points of view considered.

Staying Power

One of the ways to measure BATNA is to figure out which parties are likely to be on the losing end if they don't participate in a negotiation. Many people have learned this lesson. When a local zoning board is meeting or when other organizations are going through the decision-making process, the folks who stay to the bitter end are more likely to have an influence on the outcome.

Trust, But ...

President Ronald Reagan said that you have to remember to "Trust, but verify." In international diplomacy, some countries' governments act more transparently than others. Diplomats may have good reason to expect compliance with agreements from countries with an open approach to government. In other cases, more closed societies may hide their actions. After agreement is reached, it is particularly important to have a way of monitoring their fulfillment of their commitments.

Unless you have an agreement in advance that someone will keep an eye on your concerns, you run the risk that your interests will be ignored. Asking someone to hold your place in line, watch your luggage at the airport, or call you on your cell phone when an important issue arises requires a meaningful amount of mutual trust. If you make an agreement before negotiation begins to have someone look out for your interests, you can strengthen your BATNA.

Assumptions

We prepare for negotiations, both formally and informally, by making assumptions about various characteristics of our negotiation partners. Formal preparation is described in far more detail in Chapters 3, 4, and 5. For purposes of this discussion, however, formal preparation involves utilizing an active pre-negotiation process to consider the elements to be discussed. Informal preparation generally happens on the fly, when you rely on your instincts and pre-existing knowledge or experience to guide your negotiating. In particular, we make assumptions about each party's walking-in BATNA. Examining the basis of those assumptions is a most important element of the formal preparation process.

As you prepare to negotiate, take your BATNA apart. Look at its elements to see where they need changing and figure out how you can make those changes before the process begins. By the same token, examine your beliefs about other parties' BATNAs before going into the bargaining process.

Changes in BATNA

When the automakers Chrysler and Daimler-Benz merged, many managers at Chrysler were under the impression that the deal was a merger of equals. As a consequence, they had reason to expect a more or less equal BATNA in their dealings with parties from the Daimler organization. During the implementation of the merger, which required a great deal of joint decision making and thus negotiation by Chrysler and Daimler elements of the new entity, it became clear that there had not been a merger of equals but rather an acquisition by Daimler-Benz. People from Chrysler discovered their BATNA was weaker than they had anticipated.

How can you strengthen your BATNA and weaken theirs?

Can you justify the assumptions that underlie your assessment of their BATNA by getting confirmation from colleagues, reading their company's annual report, or doing some investigation using third parties?

Remember the distinction between walking-in BATNA and the dynamic BATNA that changes during negotiation as you gain information. If you are prepared for change, you are less likely to be thrown off by surprises and more likely to know when it's time to rely on your own resources rather than waste your time on an unpromising negotiation. Knowledge of when it's appropriate to walk away from negotiation can make the whole process work far better for you and bring you further toward reaching your objectives and satisfying your interests.

Keep your eye on the moving, dynamic BATNA. If nothing changes it during the negotiation, perhaps the negotiation itself is not the best way to solve your problem.

Manager's Checklist for Chapter 2

❏ Your BATNA, your Best Alternative To a Negotiated Agreement, tells you whether a particular negotiation is worth undertaking or continuing in light of the alternative ways you might serve your interests.

❏ Your walking-in BATNA consists of the resources over which you have control or influence that can be used to help you meet your goals and serve your interests. As the negotiation goes forward, each time you learn something new, your BATNA may change. Thus, your walking-in BATNA becomes a dynamic element during the negotiation process.

❏ BATNA can be used as a measure of the balance of power among negotiating parties. Keeping an eye on how BATNAs change during the negotiating process gives you a measure of the modifications in your relative power.

❏ The better you understand your BATNA—and the BATNA of other parties—the better you are able to judge whether to continue the negotiation or to walk away before an unappealing agreement is reached.

❏ BATNAs are made up of a variety of elements. These can include deadlines, alternatives such as other suppliers or customers, your own resources, their resources, information you gain before and during the negotiation, the level of experience you or other parties have, your interests and other parties' interests, and knowledge about the matters under consideration.

❏ You need to figure out how you can strengthen your BATNA and weaken the BATNA of other parties in order to make the balance of power more favorable to yourself.

Are We Ready? Inoculation Protects the Parties

*What convinces is conviction. Believe in the argument
you are advancing. If you don't, you're as good as dead.*
—Lyndon B. Johnson

A negotiator who is not familiar with the subject matter of the negotiation or who is required to utilize the approach that he or she has been told to use may find it difficult to proceed with enthusiasm or confidence. To protect ourselves from making mistakes in negotiation as well as to boost our confidence, we need to inoculate ourselves before we sally forth. The inoculation process can cover a variety of elements:

- We may need to learn more about the substance of the issues to be discussed.
- Our understanding of the history between the parties may need to be enhanced.
- We may need to be sold on the objectives we're pursuing in order to be more convincing to others.

To increase your comfort level and commitment to the

Inoculation The process of preparing for the negotiation process in order to commit ourselves to our strategies, objectives, and interests. In a different context, youngsters are inoculated against childhood diseases. In negotiation, inoculation for the focus of the discussion, the relationship of the parties, and the objectives of the negotiation process can protect us against surprises, keep us from saying the wrong thing, and make us more confident about achieving our goals.

objectives of your intended negotiation, you need to give yourself a shot in the arm. For the inoculation to succeed, determine whether your intended approach is likely to yield results that meet your underlying interests.

Substantive Inoculation: Knowing the Subject

It is critical to do your homework on the issues thoroughly; the more you understand, the less likely you'll be surprised or stymied by questions other parties ask. You can feel very foolish if you can't respond to questions about the specifications of a product you are selling—or if you don't know enough about a product or service you are buying to be able to measure whether what a vendor is offering will fill the bill or fit your budget.

Since making choices among alternatives is a critical element in negotiation, having information about the available choices makes a lot of sense. We need to inoculate ourselves with information ahead of time, even if most of what we learn is that we

Know Your Subject Matter

Going into a business meeting without having a good idea of what is likely to be discussed weakens your ability to negotiate effectively. When a potential customer asks about the capacity of your company's Model 5C front-end loader (even if you have come to sell a bulldozer), unless you know the answer to her question, she may doubt the information you are able to provide. While admitting ignorance because you are unfamiliar with that product line may get you past the immediate problem, you had better come back to her with the information as quickly as possible.

need to use the negotiation process to gather information that will help us reach a wise result. The negotiation process itself is an exchange of information that helps the parties reach a mutually acceptable agreement.

In Negotiation, the Past Has No Future

Too often negotiations break down into arguments about who's at fault if a hostile situation develops. We can think of numerous examples in world politics where hurts that go back many centuries are used as the excuse for barbarity. Spending time determining who the bad guys were 500 years ago may satisfy some parties' emotions, but you can't change history and generally can't change aggrieved parties' view of who did what to whom. Focusing on the past is not likely to make the future any better. To bring healing that endures, act in ways that demonstrate good faith and increase confidence between parties so that they can ultimately reach a wise agreement about the future.

Don't Let the Past Govern

In negotiation, the past has no future. The purpose of negotiation is to create for the future, not to find ways to let the wrongs of history govern our lives.

In negotiation, it is important to have as clear a sense as possible about the history between the parties so that you can recognize words or actions that may become hot button issues that could derail forward progress. Taking a look at the history of the relationship between the parties, whether they be individuals or companies, can help negotiators inoculate themselves against surprises, prevent them from making inaccurate assumptions, and avoid words or actions that will distract

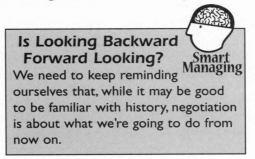

Is Looking Backward Forward Looking?

Smart Managing

We need to keep reminding ourselves that, while it may be good to be familiar with history, negotiation is about what we're going to do from now on.

other parties from the crucial issues about which they can actually make a difference.

Selling the Product to the Salesperson

Good preparation begins when we examine our reasons for pursuing the objectives we have been assigned, as well as what interests underlie the objectives we have decided on for ourselves. If we cannot sell those desired results to ourselves, how will we be able to sell them to others?

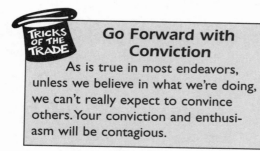

Go Forward with Conviction

As is true in most endeavors, unless we believe in what we're doing, we can't really expect to convince others. Your conviction and enthusiasm will be contagious.

Preparation in any business negotiation is especially important. Are you convinced that your assignment will be good for your career? What if the objectives you're being asked to pursue yield short-term benefits that could be unfavorable to your company in the long run? Be sure to get answers to your questions and find ways of overcoming your doubts.

Facing Up to the Boss

One of the greatest challenges many people face is being honest with a boss who's given you an assignment with which you are uncomfortable. You can't simply say to your boss, "You're out of your mind, no one will buy this approach!" However, it is perfectly appropriate to say, "I want to do a good job in the negotiation on this issue. Could you give me good arguments to use to make my points? How can I counter questions about our product quality or price? Is there anything you know about the folks I'll be dealing with that may help me do a better job of interacting with them?"

You don't want to convey the message that you're ignorant or incompetent; if you do that, your boss may ask why he or she has given you the job in the first place. If you ask searching questions that require detailed answers, you demonstrate that you want to do a better job and represent your company or division to maximum effect.

Goals of Inoculation

By being well prepared before negotiation, you enter the process with greater confidence and greater competence. Both confidence and competence communicate themselves to the parties with whom you are negotiating. It makes you more believable and more likely to convince others to agree with you.

Sometimes the most important inoculation takes place within our own organizations, whether our section of a business, our family, or any other group we depend on to implement any agreement we reach with "outsiders." Our credibility is at risk if we sell a deal to a customer and then other divisions tell us that our price, delivery date, or specifications are out of line. We need to bring our colleagues into the process before we venture into negotiation outside our team to make sure that we can deliver what we intend to offer.

To be certain that your colleagues will be committed to deliver what you promise, they, too, must be inoculated before formal negotiations begin. In addi-

> **Tribalism**
>
> When you negotiate as a representative of a group of stakeholders or constituencies, consider the impact of your actions on those stakeholders. Within many companies, separate tribes may have different goals. While people in sales are looking at one set of numbers, people in manufacturing or purchasing are concerned with very different goals. Make sure you're aware of the needs of all the stakeholders who will be affected by the negotiation.

Smart Managing

tion, owners of the business, customers, government regulators, and other parties such as consumer interest groups or businesses that may gain or lose business depending on the outcome of your negotiations may need to be convinced that the course of action you're pursuing is favorable to their interests.

Inoculation as a Tool for Improving Your BATNA

As indicated in Chapter 2, you need to be aware of your BATNA (Best Alternative To a Negotiated Agreement) at all points in the negotiation process. Your walking-in BATNA—the BATNA with which you start out—may appear to consist of one set of elements at the outset. As you go through the inoculation process, learning more about the subject matter of the negotiation, the history of the relationship of the parties, and the decision-influ-

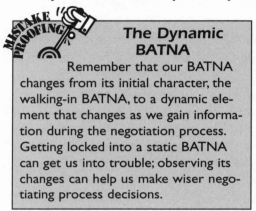

The Dynamic BATNA

Remember that our BATNA changes from its initial character, the walking-in BATNA, to a dynamic element that changes as we gain information during the negotiation process. Getting locked into a static BATNA can get us into trouble; observing its changes can help us make wiser negotiating process decisions.

encing points that will lead you toward a favorable result, you learn more about your BATNA. The knowledge you gain may give you ideas for improving your BATNA even before negotiation begins. Additional knowledge may also help you think of ways to weaken the BATNA of the parties with whom you'll be negotiating to help tilt the balance of power toward yourself.

The process of inoculating your colleagues can play a critical role in opening doors to strengthening your BATNA. Their knowledge about the substantive issues, the parties with whom you are about to negotiate, or other factors that may influence the outcome can be extremely helpful. Moreover, since that internal inoculation process should yield greater buy-in from your colleagues, it means that their increased support itself strengthens your BATNA.

What Information Do We Need About Ourselves?

It is easy to fall into the trap of thinking, "If I want it, it must be a good objective," or "It must be the best way to accomplish the goals of my company or myself." Although it takes considerable effort, it is crucial to examine why a particular solution or a particular approach is better than another.

We need to have a clear sense of our interests when we are pursuing a raise at work. Do we need more money to change

> ## Understanding Your Real Interests
> You may decide you need a vacation and immediately choose a familiar place where lots of people you know are likely to be found. However, you need to look more deeply at the choices available to you and why you make them. If the purpose of the vacation is to relax, a place that offers an active social life may not be the right answer. If the vacation is intended to give you a chance to reconnect with your wife or husband—or children—you need to consider what sort of location and what sort of facilities will make the most sense. Renting a cottage on a lake may be a great break for a person who likes to fish; it may not sound like much of a break for someone who is sick of cooking or making beds.

our standard of living? Will the money demonstrate that our employer values us more this year than last year? As we look at this, we can develop a greater understanding of whether our ego can be served by a larger office or a parking space or a fancy title. Perhaps we need the raise as a reward for continuing in a job that creates high stress and little satisfaction. If we look at the situation in that light, our interest might better be served looking for a different job rather than getting more money without an improvement in the quality of our work life.

By examining the reasons behind what we want, we develop a clearer understanding of what is truly important to us. That

> ## Inoculation Is Understanding
> **Smart Managing**
> The better you understand the situation, the better inoculated you are against surprise and miscalculation of the best solution to a problem. Prepare yourself well. It can make all the difference.

greater understanding is another form of inoculation, providing us a better sense of how to negotiate and how the variety of solutions to the issues we're facing will serve our interests. If someone's ego is a higher-ranked interest than money in the bank, a compensation package reflecting that ranking is more likely to result if that individual has reached that understanding of his or her interests.

What Information Do We Need About Other Parties?

The more we understand the interests that lie behind the positions of the people with whom we're negotiating, the less likely we'll be surprised by issues they raise. When it comes to understanding other parties better, inoculation efforts should be aimed at vaccinating ourselves against anything we might not expect. If we learn that someone with whom we'll be negotiating is a real bureaucrat, that takes us part of the distance. Further research that tells us he is threatened by change or modifications because he suffered some sort of trauma in a prior job can help us understand how to deal with him.

Grandpa Was Always Early

For years I used to wonder why my Grandfather was always early for every appointment—business or social. I later learned that he had been fired from his first job, working on the subway in New York City, for being late. We developed a habit of inviting him to show up at family events about 45 minutes after everyone else was asked to get there. As a consequence, he tended to show up on time rather than embarrassingly early.

Preparing for Negotiation on Your Own

One of the more significant risks we take in the inoculation process is concluding that we know all the answers, that we are totally prepared for anything that may come from another party. While our preparation work gives us greater understanding of the overall context in which a negotiation will take place, we have to be careful not to believe that all our assumptions are correct. Our assumptions have to be tested. One of the ways we should view the negotiation process is as an information-gathering activity that lets us know whether the assumptions we have adopted are accurate or not.

As you prepare for negotiation, you may not understand all the factors that are important to other parties. As a result, you will be forced to make assumptions. You have the freedom to

---

Assumptions

None of us knows everything; often the best we can do is make assumptions based on our best estimates about other parties. Remembering that assumptions are not demonstrated facts, can protect us from locking ourselves into a positional approach in the negotiation process. When we recognize we are working with assumptions, rather than with proven facts, we can use the negotiation process as a means for reality testing and improve our understanding of what will influence other parties.

---

make a broad range of assumptions, but each one must be carefully tested as you learn more about the actual interests of the parties as well as the underlying interests of their constituencies.

Active Listening

Using negotiation as a mechanism for gathering information requires an appropriate balance between the two sides of communication: presenting and receiving. Your search for information is best achieved by asking open-ended questions and then disciplining yourself to listen closely and carefully to the answers those questions yield. Rather than asking your customer, "Do you like this product?" it can make more sense to ask, "How would you describe the product to your design group?" The first question is likely to yield a "Yes" or "No" and not give you much information. Your customer's answer to the second question should give you a clearer sense of his or her objectives and interests.

Listening requires a great deal of self-discipline. Most of us can't wait for other folks to finish talking so that we can zap them with a brilliant comeback. We may appear to be listening, but too often we are using bits and

Failing to Listen

Asking a question and ignoring the answer is like searching for buried treasure and then abandoning it once you find out where it is. By listening closely to what others tell you, you can learn more not only about their interests and needs but enlighten your own proposal development as well.

Self-Control

TRICKS OF THE TRADE

Perhaps the starkest way to comprehend how to listen is to follow the rule used at a friend's family dinner table: Only one person is allowed to be angry at a time. If I answer your anger with my anger, the emotional level of the communication escalates, most likely wiping out the substance of whatever may be under discussion. In these situations, we need to recognize just whose turn it is to be angry. If it is not our turn, we have to keep our emotions under control, reminding ourselves from time to time, "It's not my turn to be angry."

pieces of what the other person is saying to formulate and reformulate our own thoughts.

When it comes to listening in negotiation, often called active listening, we may not have to keep our emotions in check, although it does make sense to keep our mouth closed and our ears open.

If we want to inoculate ourselves with information before negotiations begin, listen to people who may not be parties to the bargain in order to learn more about the folks with whom we'll be trying to reach a decision. It makes sense to check around with people who've negotiated before with the parties we're about to meet, to find out whether any of our colleagues has information to offer, or to check on other negotiators' reputations within a trade association to help draw a more complete picture of their approach to negotiation.

KEY TERM

Active listening Since information is the fundamental asset of negotiation, the better we listen, the better we'll negotiate. Active listening requires paying full attention to other parties rather than focusing on ourselves.

The same is certainly true when it comes to your communication with your negotiation partners; the information they supply during the negotiation process can give you tools and ideas to use as the negotiation goes forward. If you listen carefully, it will help strengthen your comprehension of the issues under discussion and will inoculate you for what is about to happen in the bargaining process. Active listening can give you a sense of the objectives or interests your counterparts will likely pursue during the negotiation. Perhaps they will reveal things you may not have considered during your preparation.

Responding to What We Learn

One of the key aims of a good negotiator is to be reasonably certain that she and her negotiation partner are on the same page. If I am focused on one set of issues and you are focused on different ones, we are not negotiating. It's similar to two railroad tracks: They run parallel for miles and miles—and never meet.

If we do a good job of active listening to colleagues and others with whom we do research while we prepare for a negotiation and during the negotiation itself, we should be able to ask the person who has been talking,

"Then if I understand you correctly, you said A, B, C, and D."

We don't want to repeat everything she said word for word, but we need to communicate as clearly as possible what

Reciprocity Can Lead to Better Negotiation
TRICKS OF THE TRADE
People aren't always accustomed to having others really pay attention to them. When you make it clear that you have been listening closely, you raise the level of civility in the conversation. The underlying statement you are making is, "Okay, I listened to you; now it is your turn to listen to me."

we have understood. When I say I understand you, that does not mean I agree with you. This point should be made diplomatically—but clearly.

The Power of Silence

Sometimes the folks with whom we negotiate present ideas with which we simply cannot agree. In that situation, it may be wisest to withhold any reaction. Treat them with what's called the Power of Silence. Although this tactic takes a great deal of self-control, it can be a most effective weapon. If you have inoculated yourself well, you will recognize that what another person says is off the charts and unacceptable. If you say, "Bill, that's the dumbest idea I ever heard," you add an emotional compo-

The Power of Silence

My favorite story of the use of silence concerns my friend Tony. Tony is a lawyer who often represents automobile insurance companies that are being sued when a policyholder has gotten into an accident. He had done a good job of research and was well-inoculated regarding a case he had been assigned. At 4:15 one afternoon, Tony called the insurance company he was representing and told the claims agent, "I've been working on the Jones case. If we offer them $60,000, I'm sure they will settle and that will save the insurance company litigation costs and the risk of a higher award if we go to court." The claims agent responded, "Your limit is $30,000!"

Tony didn't say anything. He switched the phone from one ear to the other and went to work on another case. Not a sound passed between the two men as the clock ticked to 4:30. Still not a word at 4:45, half an hour after the phone call had begun. At 5:00, Tony could hear sounds in the background at the other end: "Good night, Charlie. See you in the morning, Charlie. Don't work too late." Still neither Tony nor Charlie said a word. Finally, at 10 minutes after 5, fully 55 minutes after the phone call had begun, Charlie said, "All right, dammit! You can offer the $60,000. But that's it!" And he slammed down the phone. By keeping silent, Tony had gotten Charlie, the claims agent, to rethink his approach and then give Tony approval for his proposed settlement.

nent to the discussion. If you sit there wearing a poker face, you can make that point quite effectively.

Inoculation Includes Process as Well as Substance

In preparing for negotiation, you need to think about the negotiation process as well as the items or ideas you plan to discuss with your negotiation partner. While some of the process issues may appear simple, they can have a significant influence on the outcome:

- Where are you going to meet?
- Will one of the negotiation partners get the home court advantage?
- If I agree to travel to your office for a meeting, that can signal that I have "given" something and it may create a

sense that you owe me something in return.

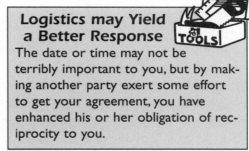

Logistics may Yield a Better Response
The date or time may not be terribly important to you, but by making another party exert some effort to get your agreement, you have enhanced his or her obligation of reciprocity to you.

The same kind of considerations apply to such issues as choice of date and time, and even decisions about the duration of a negotiation session or the whole negotiation process. Who is "giving in" on what may appear to be trivial issues? One hint to keep in mind is that if you do acquiesce on date or time, you may want to do so only after the person with whom you'll be negotiating has had to convince you to do so.

Agendas

Part of the preparation for negotiation can include agreeing on the agenda of items you are planning to discuss. Here again, your preparatory or inoculation work can be significant in influencing the outcome. You need to think about what you are prepared to discuss as well as the order in which those issues should be raised.

- Will it be more advantageous to start with the easy matters and work up to the harder issues?
- Should you get the tough issues out of the way first?
- What about mixing the order?

Changing Priorities During Negotiation

TRICKS OF THE TRADE

Some negotiators bargain early over issues that are not terribly important to them. They utilize a strategy in which they do some hard bargaining, hoping to "win" on those particular elements of the agreement. Then, sometime later in the negotiation process, they reach an issue of far greater importance to them. They might say, "You know, I was quite pleased you agreed to give me what I wanted on issue D. But now that I think of it, issue M is so important to me that I'm prepared to give back what you gave up on issue D if you will agree to my proposal on issue M."

Agreeing on the agenda ahead of time with your negotiation partner can bring a series of advantages to each party. You have an opportunity to learn about one another's priorities. You find out about issues that will be discussed, thus protecting yourself that much more against surprises. You may learn about an issue another party wants to raise in time to get better prepared on it yourself. You can check company policy or other sources of information to inoculate yourself on a broader range of issues. As you cooperate in the development of the agenda, you and the other negotiators are getting into the habit of agreeing with each other on apparently trivial issues. Becoming comfortable with the idea that you and the other parties can agree can make the negotiation itself proceed far more smoothly.

Internal and External Inoculation

This chapter focuses a great deal on how and why we want to inoculate *ourselves* to gain greater understanding about the subject matter, the people with whom we're negotiating, and the negotiation process itself. In addition, it is important to consider how inoculating other parties to the negotiation can make the process yield a wiser, more satisfying result.

Internal Inoculation

Clearly, just as we have to inoculate ourselves, we need to make sure our colleagues, teammates, or family are on the same page.

Involving your colleagues is necessary if you are to depend on their buy-in to deals you hope to make. Before making a sale, purchase, or other bargain, learn whether what you would like to deliver reflects reality as

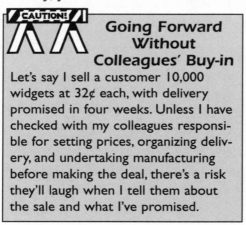

CAUTION!

Going Forward Without Colleagues' Buy-in

Let's say I sell a customer 10,000 widgets at 32¢ each, with delivery promised in four weeks. Unless I have checked with my colleagues responsible for setting prices, organizing delivery, and undertaking manufacturing before making the deal, there's a risk they'll laugh when I tell them about the sale and what I've promised.

they see it. They need to be inoculated regarding the deal ahead of time, not after the fact.

External Inoculation

When we are negotiating with parties with whom we have an ongoing relationship, generally speaking inoculation is a normal result of the interaction among us. Negotiations with new parties, however, require inoculation as an independent precursor to the bargaining process. One of the questions we need to ask is whether the people who are doing the negotiating have the authority to make decisions as well as fulfill any promises that are made. We need to be able to convince the parties to a negotiation that it is appropriate for them to spend time dealing with us in order to reach a satisfactory agreement. Before beginning a negotiation, we should be thinking of ways to convince others that we have both the responsibility and the authority to make a deal.

All of these issues need to be examined before negotiations begin as part of our inoculation process. The better we understand our strengths and weaknesses as deal makers, the greater the likelihood that what we *don't* say will underscore what we *do* say as the negotiation goes forward. The inoculation process must include

Make Yourself Credible

Arriving with a letter signed by your CEO indicating your deal-making power is probably overkill, but you might consider letting other parties know about your experience with other similar deals. Speak knowledgeably about the substantive and logistical issues and express yourself clearly when it comes to decision making. If your decision-making power is limited, honesty may increase another party's willingness to trust your word. Being clear about your company's decision-making process gives others more confidence in what you say.

whatever research might be needed to help us understand our capacity to decide and to act as we negotiate and fulfill the elements of agreements we reach.

The Bottom Line

We are not fully inoculated until we understand the bottom line of our bargaining efforts.

Our bottom line is not our BATNA, but rather the limits there may be to deals we can make. When my wife and I buy a car, there is a limit on how much we can spend—that is our bottom line. Our BATNA could be that there are several dealers of comparable cars within 20 miles of our home. We may be able to foster competition among those dealers to get the best price.

> **Key Term**
>
> **Bottom line** The points beyond which we cannot go. There are some goals that must be achieved. These can be considered elements of our bottom line. Offering to buy raw materials at a price that exceeds the production budget may price the ultimate product out of the market and make it impossible for your company to sell its goods. You need to know the maximum you can spend for the raw materials: that is your bottom line.

Understanding our bottom line is an important factor in the overall package we need to prepare before negotiations begin.

While price may be the simplest example of a bottom line, other factors involving such issues as quality of life may well determine just how far we're willing to go to reach a deal. Knowing this ahead of time can help us negotiate far more intelligently and effectively.

When Inoculation Is Impossible

We can't inoculate ourselves before every negotiation. Sometimes there's no warning that a negotiation is about to happen. We pick up the phone, step out into the corridor, or—to use the 1950s television sitcom archetype—walk into our house only to hear our spouse say to one of the kids, "I warned you what would happen when Daddy got home!" Getting used to inoculating ourselves before negotiation helps build the instincts we need in order to be effective negotiators. Practicing the discipline of inoculation can be critical to our success when we haven't had time to fully prepare.

Manager's Checklist for Chapter 3

❑ Try to know as much as possible about the subject matter of the negotiation ahead of time. Think of this as an inoculation to prepare you for questions from other negotiators—and to protect you from surprises.

❑ Unless someone selling an idea or product is enthusiastic about it, she will have a much more difficult time engendering enthusiasm on the part of other parties.

❑ Inoculation with as much information as possible not only informs you about your BATNA, it can also help you figure out how to make it stronger.

❑ As part of your inoculation process, understanding what interests underlie your objectives—and what interests underlie the objectives of other negotiators—increases the likelihood that you'll negotiate with confidence and competence.

❑ The best way to get good information throughout the negotiation process is to use active listening. This should begin as you inoculate yourself to build your comfort with the objectives and interests you will be pursuing in the negotiation.

❑ You need to consider the negotiation process as well as the subject matter as you inoculate yourself. Consider the effect of choices of time and place, the importance of the relationship between you and other negotiators, and how your focus on interests should be used in the negotiation process.

❑ Setting the agenda ahead of time, ideally in cooperation with other parties, will give you foreknowledge that should aid your negotiation and inoculate you against surprise issues.

❑ Your preliminary work with colleagues within your team or from other sections of your organization will increase your subject matter knowledge and increase the likelihood that your colleagues will support the agreement you reach through negotiation. Unless there is good internal negotiation that brings colleagues together on the same page, external negotiations can be quite risky.

❏ Understanding your bottom line—and how it differs from your BATNA—is a critical part of your inoculation process.

❏ Getting into the habit of inoculating yourself before negotiations can help you deal more effectively with negotiations for which you have not had time to plan.

Preparation Part One: Stakeholders, Constituents, and Interests

In real estate, the three most important words are "location, location, location."

In negotiation, the three most important words are "preparation, preparation, preparation."

Shooting from the Hip

Some people see themselves as instinctive or natural negotiators. Their instinctive approach to negotiation may very well yield favorable results. In spite of the possibility that a negotiator may be quite good at hitting the target shooting from the hip, however, there is always the chance that his or her aim may not be perfect. And other people on the negotiating team may not feel the same level of confidence in their negotiating ability. In extreme examples, this is sometimes referred to as negotiation phobia. Someone who approaches negotiation lacking confidence in his ability to make effective use of the process has an especially strong need to prepare. Gambling that he can negotiate effectively by going with the flow is a risky proposition.

Unplanned Negotiations

Very often we are faced with negotiating when we least expect it. We run into negotiations we have not anticipated when we answer the phone, step out of our offices, or bump into a colleague on the street. If we are accustomed to preparing for negotiation, we are more likely to have developed instincts to help us cope with unexpected negotiations.

Smart Managing

Build Your Instincts with Preparation

Since we can't always prepare for every negotiation, it is important to prepare as much as possible when we do have the opportunity. The habit of good preparation builds instincts that will help us negotiate when we don't have time to prepare for an unexpected negotiation.

Surprises

There are times when even the best instinctive negotiators find themselves surprised by something another negotiator says or does. Being on the receiving end of a surprise can throw even the best negotiator. If you haven't considered a possibility presented by your negotiation partner—someone with whom you are negotiating in order to reach an agreement—it may take time and recalculation to figure out how the unexpected offer fits with your interests. When you are undergoing your annual personnel review and your primary focus is on how much your bonus will be, it can be unsettling if your boss unexpectedly asks you to provide your analysis of the performance of other people in your department. How will your comments affect your bonus? If you say only good things about your

Mistake Proofing

You Can't Plan for Everything

You cannot anticipate everything another party may say. Life would be boring if every human interaction went exactly as predicted. Nonetheless, thinking ahead of time about the widest possible variety of issues that may arise during negotiations can help your on-the-spot analyses of how various proposals might affect the outcome of the negotiation.

colleagues, can you count on their doing so in your behalf? If all your comments on others are favorable, what will that do to your credibility and your short- and long-term interests?

What Does Preparation Mean?

In warfare, General Dwight Eisenhower said, "Before a battle, preparation is everything. Once the battle has begun, preparation is nothing." That statement is fundamentally misleading. While negotiation is certainly not combat, we need to look at Eisenhower's words very carefully. Preparation is the process of assembling information and/or materials to enable you to carry out a task. It is easy enough to tell Eisenhower's ghost that unless his forces prepared for battle with sufficient materials— from weapons to first aid supplies—the risk to his troops was enormous. Unless preparation has been well done, it will have a definitive impact on the outcome of the combat. You cannot be certain whether any preparation you do will cover all the issues that may arise in a negotiation. Failing to prepare and leaving everything to chance is far more risky than doing your best to be ready. In negotiation, particularly when we are aiming for the goal of a mutually created agreement that the parties will fulfill willingly, good preparation can make a tremendous difference.

You need to prepare colleagues within your company so that you will not present them with an unattractive negotiated result. Be careful not to raise your colleagues' expectations to an unre-

---

Negotiation Prep

Tools to include in preparing for a negotiation:
- Understand your interests.
- Think about other parties' BATNAs. While you cannot know another party's BATNA, good preparation involves thinking about the elements that other parties' BATNAs may include. The negotiation process involves testing the reality of your assumptions about both your own BATNA and those of other parties.
- Know about the subject matter of the negotiation.
- Know about the parties with whom you're going to negotiate.

alistic level. Your input combined with what you learn from your colleagues can help everyone develop expectations that reflect likely results rather than pie-in-the-sky hopes. It also makes sense to consider how you might prepare your counterparts for the process; for example, letting them know ahead of time that you need some specific data means you won't embarrass them during the negotiation process by asking questions to which they don't have answers.

Looking Inside Yourself

Your first preparatory step may possibly be the most difficult—developing an understanding of the interests that are driving the decision making you'll be doing in the negotiation process. Examining your objectives requires figuring out which are positions and which are interests. Which interest needs to be met in order for you to be able to move toward the next interest? Can you assign a priority to your interests? Is one interest the most important of all, the fundamental interest?

The challenge you face in determining whether something you're pursuing is an interest or a position is no joke. It is easy to fall into the trap of thinking, "If that's what I want, there must be a good reason for it." Unless you understand the reason why something is worth negotiating for, you may not rec-

Prioritizing Your Interests

If your boss assigns you to make a deal, what are your interests in the successful fulfillment of that assignment? You want to satisfy your boss—but is that because you want a raise, a promotion, a job change that needs to be earned by a specific accomplishment? Do you want to make your boss look good, no matter whether it helps your own career aspirations or not? Does the deal you're assigned to make hold the promise of increasing the value of the shares you have in your company? Will this particular negotiation help solidify the business relationship you have with another party? Examine each of these interests and understand their relative priority. When you have a good sense of where you're coming from, you'll have a better sense of how to get where you want to go.

ognize when other parties offer ways to get there that you haven't thought of yourself. Preparing by understanding and prioritizing your interests provides you with benchmarks for measuring whether a particular solution brings you closer to or keeps you away from achieving your goals. Your list of interests may include being able to buy a vacation house to which you can ultimately retire, increasing your financial resources through salary and other benefits, having a workload that does not present too much conflict with your family life, negotiating deals that make you look good in terms of your boss's and company's priorities, and retaining good relationships with suppliers or customers. This mixture of personal and professional interests needs to be prioritized. Decide where you need to put the most effort at the right time in order to satisfy the largest possible proportion of your interests.

Understanding the Subject Matter

As you negotiate, your preparation to familiarize yourself with the ideas, specifications, and other elements of the issues to be decided gives you considerably greater power in the negotiation process. It may or may not change your BATNA, but it will certainly change your comfort with the discussions that constitute the negotiation.

You can learn about the subject matter by reading, asking knowledgeable colleagues, or depending on other experts for advice. Your knowledge is increased if you are famil-

> **The Need for Information** CAUTION!
>
> Information is the fundamental asset in negotiation. If you don't have the information that you need, you are seriously handicapped.

iar with the use of the item or information at stake in the negotiation. Knowing that a certain type of plastic doesn't work at high temperatures can protect you from creating a class of irate customers who've ruined meals using the wrong container in their microwave ovens. While the issues you face are not always that simple, the lesson is clear: The better you understand what

Knowledge Brings Confidence

The confidence you feel as you enter negotiations involving familiar subject matter can communicate itself to your negotiation partners as well as to members of your own team. If you are credible, people will take what you say seriously. When someone can tell you don't know what you're talking about, the chance that you'll be able to convince that person of anything is weak.

you're dealing with, the less likely you are to make mistakes.

Internal Negotiations

Negotiations within your organization are often far more important than negotiations you undertake with outsiders. To make a successful sale, for example, you must first negotiate with your colleagues regarding price, specifications, and delivery. You need to know what promises you can make and keep. Your colleagues are far more likely to be cooperative in fulfilling their obligations under an agreement you reach if they feel you have considered their concerns.

Know What Promises You Can Deliver

If you make a deal with a customer without consulting your colleagues and then tell them what you've agreed to have them do, they may present some obstacles to implementing your deal. Understanding your company's capacity to deliver a variety of elements as part of a deal, finding out the importance of particular specifications, or getting a sense of deadlines or pressures different segments of your company face can make the difference between negotiating a wise agreement and ending up with egg on your face.

Members of the home team cannot be taken for granted—whether they are folks at work or members of your family. As playwright Arthur Miller wrote in his drama, *Death of a Salesman*, "Attention must be paid." Whether it is your co-workers' egos or the company's cash flow, unless you pay serious attention to relevant interests of the people who will derive positive or negative consequences from the agreement you reach through negotiation, you are risking an uncooperative response.

Another reason for taking internal negotiations seriously is to arrive at buy-in. Just as you want the outside parties with whom you negotiate to buy into the ultimate agreement, getting your co-workers to feel ownership of the agreement is critical for its fulfillment.

Preparing Other Parties

We have to pay particularly close attention to how much we want to prepare with our negotiation counterparts before starting the actual process. In the experience of most sophisticated negotiation professionals, interest-based collaborative negotiation is likely to lead to a wise result. However, we have to be careful to distinguish between the approach that says we should lay all our cards on the table and the more realistic conclusion that other parties may not care about the same things we do.

Rather than working on preparation with your negotiation partners by simply doing an information dump, work on reaching agreement about the process and making sure you share a desire to discuss the same subject matter.

> **When to Be Quiet** ⚠️CAUTION!
>
> Good salespeople know that when people start to agree with you, it's time to stop talking. Offering too much information can turn into overselling, which will turn off potential customers. In negotiation, information overload can confuse parties and impede the likelihood of achieving a clear mutual understanding.

Preparing for the Process

After you have figured out with whom you want to negotiate, how you initiate communication requires some thought. For purposes of this section, we have assumed that the other negotiators are willing to meet with you—you do not face the problem of getting your foot in the door. While a phone call or e-mail saying, "I would like to get together with you to discuss the Acme situation," is succinct and reasonably clear, it is only an offer to begin the negotiation process. Contrast this to an open-

Logistics Can Influence the Process

Smart Managing   Explore the logistics. By agreeing to meet at another party's office, you may be feeding their ego and creating a feeling in that person that he owes you something in return, an obligation of reciprocity. Setting up meetings in a world where people have to travel significant distances can require careful consideration of logistics, comfort, and access to resources for decision making. A party's BATNA may be affected by the deadlines implicit in having to meet a particular plane schedule.

ing that says, "The Acme situation requires the following resources and commitments from our companies. Let's set up a timetable for each of us to take the appropriate steps."

In this case you're opening with a conclusion, telling the other party what you think, and, by implication, what they should think. This is not negotiation; it is giving orders.

If your counterpart does, indeed, want to meet about Acme, the next step for you to take involves asking questions:

- When and where shall we meet?
- Is there information I may have that you feel can help us reach the best agreement?
- How much time do you think we should allocate to our decision-making process?

Preparing on the Substance: Subject Matter of the Negotiation

Going to a meeting only to discover that the parties have contrary expectations about what is to be discussed or the order in which issues will be raised can be frustrating. One preventative move is to arrange for preparatory communication about the issues that will appear on the agenda of your meeting.

You can learn a great deal of information about where another person is coming from when you undertake collaborative agenda preparation. If you want to discuss one issue at the very beginning of the process and your negotiation partner feels it belongs in the middle or at the end of the agenda, consider what that tells you about his or her priorities. You might even

Joint Agenda Preparation

Working together on the agenda brings a number of bene- **Smart Managing**
fits: In addition to assuring that the right parties are meeting,
shared agenda preparation can clarify the subject matter so that parties will have a common agreement about what issues will be raised.
Moreover, if the agenda process gives the parties an opportunity to
practice reaching agreement in a situation where the stakes are lower
than the actual negotiation, it can increase the chances that all parties
will develop a process for reaching agreement when the rubber hits
the road.

ask the question, "Why do you feel that discussing issue X at
the beginning is a good idea?"

The answer may tell you that you need to do additional subject matter preparation, or that you need to prepare yourself
with more knowledge about the interests of your negotiation
partner, or that your BATNA is likely to be called into play and
negotiating with that particular party may not be as productive
as you might wish.

Juggling Conflicting Agendas

As you and your counterparts exchange ideas about the elements of the agenda of your negotiation, you have already
begun the actual process of negotiation. Like organizing the
logistical elements of your interaction, your efforts to develop
an agenda offer the parties an opportunity to practice reaching
agreement.

If there are problems agreeing on an agenda, working them
out is real-world negotiation. It will help you learn more about
the priorities of other parties' interests and also give you an idea
of hot button issues. You will discover where there is likely to be
common ground and whether there are areas where you need
to be prepared to modify your expectations about the process
or the possible outcome of the negotiations.

How you and your negotiation partner, the person with
whom you hope to reach agreement, resolve differences over

the agenda can also set the tone of how differences are resolved in the actual negotiation process. The relative strength of each party's BATNA may well have an impact on who "gives" on what issue. The understanding you gain in this preparation for negotiation will hint at what may need changing in your BATNA, your understanding of the subject matter, or your expectations in terms of meeting your interests.

Strengthening and Weakening BATNAs

With that information in hand, you need to add another job to your preparation: figuring out how to strengthen your own BATNA and/or weaken the BATNA of the others. Ask yourself a variety of questions:

- How can I increase my capacity to resolve the issue independently, without the help of other parties?
- What resources do I need?
- Are there resources currently available to me that need to be modified to increase the likelihood that I can take care of things without needing the cooperation of others to get my interests met?"

Preparation to Clarify Your BATNA

The more you learn before negotiation, the better you'll understand your initial, walking-in BATNA. Your preparation will also increase your comprehension of the BATNAs of other parties. Finding out about what kinds of deadlines they face, discovering whether they can choose to work with one of your competitors, or learning about how your product or its price stacks up against others in the market will give you a better sense of other parties' BATNAs.

At the same time, you need to prepare yourself by determining ways to convince the other parties that they cannot solve their problems or fulfill their interests without your help. If you face competition, what do you need to do to increase your value in the minds of your negotiation partners, the people with whom you want to reach agreement? How can you make your competitors look less appealing? Do you have a unique selling proposition that will appeal to a potential client based on what they've revealed in agenda discussions? Are there other ways to learn about their interests so that you can characterize your proposals in ways that demonstrate that doing business with you is far more likely to yield the results they desire than they are likely to get from your competition or from other approaches to getting the job done?

Reasons to Prepare for Negotiation

One of the things you are looking for in the preparation process is an indication of what is going to be important and/or relevant in reaching decisions that make sense to the negotiating parties, including yourself. On top of that, good preparation will give you a roadmap outlining the information you need to uncover during the negotiation process. Not only will this give you direction, it will also increase the likely efficiency of the negotiation process.

Fundamentally, a good job of preparation will make you more competent to negotiate on a given range of issues with a given set of parties. Knowing that you are well prepared will increase your self-confidence and help you enter the negotiation process with a sense of relative calm—an air of being unflappable. If you have prepared well, odds are that you won't be surprised and won't fear losing your cool during the negotiations.

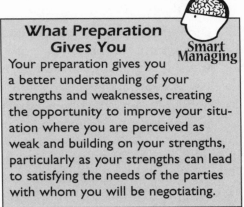

What Preparation Gives You

Smart Managing

Your preparation gives you a better understanding of your strengths and weaknesses, creating the opportunity to improve your situation where you are perceived as weak and building on your strengths, particularly as your strengths can lead to satisfying the needs of the parties with whom you will be negotiating.

Manager's Checklist for Chapter 4

❑ Relying strictly on instinct when you're negotiating is very risky. Not knowing much about the subject matter of the negotiation or having a fuzzy sense of the interests of the parties may lead you to do or say things you regret. You don't want to slap yourself on the forehead after the agreement is signed and say, "Darn, I forgot about the delivery schedule!"

❑ You cannot always prepare for negotiations. Sometimes they just happen when you bump into business colleagues unexpectedly. Developing the habit of preparing for negotiations increases the likelihood that you'll enhance instincts that will help you in unplanned negotiations.

❑ Preparing for negotiation by considering the issues other parties may raise can help you cope with surprises. Even if you've dismissed those possible issues, just thinking about them ahead of time can be helpful.

❑ You can't prepare for anything and everything. However, if you think ahead, you're likely to be able to negotiate more effectively.

❑ The hardest part of preparation is understanding and prioritizing your interests. You need to figure out how specific goals or objectives serve interests and whether your problem-solving approach is really the only one that will work.

❑ In order to be credible to others, as well as more confident as a negotiator, do meticulous homework on the subject matter likely to be treated during the negotiation. If others think you don't know what you're talking about, they won't take your input seriously.

❑ Working within your organization can be the most rewarding part of preparation. It will increase your co-workers' belief that you take them seriously, offer you their perspectives on what can be delivered, and enhance the likelihood that your colleagues will buy into the agreement you deliver as a result of your external negotiations.

❏ In addition to preparing yourself and your co-workers, it's a good idea to prepare the parties with whom you'll be negotiating—your negotiation partners. Giving them a heads up on upcoming issues is good manners and increases the likelihood that they'll have accurate information at their fingertips.

❏ Different parties have different reasons for negotiating. Figuring out how the varying interests can be used in a complementary manner to yield an agreement that each party will willingly fulfill is easier if you've considered them in advance.

❏ Your preparation should increase your understanding of your walking-in BATNA and the elements of other parties' BATNAs. Think of how you can strengthen your BATNA before you walk into the negotiation and how you can weaken other parties' BATNAs so that they need your cooperation more.

❏ Preparation is the foundation for a good negotiation process. It increases your confidence and competence, offers protection against nasty surprises, and enhances the likelihood that you'll be able to make a deal that responds to more parties' interests. Preparation can form the basis for a wise agreement.

Preparation Part Two: Developing a Strategy Using Interest Mapping

You can't tell the players without a scorecard.
—old sports saying

Making Assumptions

As you prepare for negotiation, you may not understand all the factors that are important to the other parties. In that case, you will be forced to make assumptions. Sometimes your assumptions are based on your own personal experience. In other situations, you have to rely on colleagues for ideas about what makes a particular party tick. You can also acquire information on which to base your assumptions from publications or from the documents about a company's history. While you have the freedom to make a broad range of assumptions, each one must be carefully tested as you learn more about the actual interests of parties to a negotiation as well as the interests of their constituencies.

Preparing for negotiation using assumptions is a critical

early step in developing your strategy and giving you a tool for doing a reality check of your assumptions. Since information is the fundamental asset in negotiation, testing the accuracy of your assumptions can provide you with the outline of the information needed to bring all parties closer to a workable and wise agreement.

Popular Culture CAUTION!

Assumptions form part of popular culture: When a person is appointed or elected to a judicial post, we often think of the term "sober as a judge." The judgeship may be considered a promotion for a person who, earlier in his or her legal career, may have been considered a "shark." We need to be cautious not to let popular culture so influence our assumptions that our analysis is governed by stereotypes rather than by the facts about real people.

Interested Parties

On some occasions, there are only two interested parties or stakeholders in a negotiation. In business, this is almost never the case; in personal life, it is exceedingly rare. When we negotiate face to face with another person, generally speaking each of us has constituencies looking over our shoulder, concerned in some way about the outcome of the negotiation. In business negotiations, our constituents or the stakeholders interested in the outcome may include bosses, peers, subordinates, shareholders, competitors, ultimate consumers of the goods or services involved in the transaction, regulators, and other businesses in the community whose well-being may be dependent on the success of our venture.

In our personal lives, the kinds of issues we negotiate may have an impact on members of our family, neighbors, or folks who have an interest in the deal you and your negotiation partner are making. When we negotiate, we must always consider who will derive some consequence as a result of the agreement we reach. Our constituents' interests may appear remote. If we ignore them, however, they may come back to haunt us when we are least expecting it.

> **Key Term**
>
> **Stakeholders** The clearest way to refer to the people who are negotiating and their various constituents or constituencies is the term *stakeholder*. Stakeholders are people or organizations who could derive some consequence from the outcome of your negotiation. While this certainly includes you and your negotiation partner, it also can include people or groups with whom none of the negotiating parties has a relationship. If you and I are collaborating on writing a Broadway musical, additional stakeholders include performers and others who will derive income from a successful production, the audience we hope to attract and entertain, and interest groups who might be concerned with how our production portrays members of certain religious or ethnic groups.

Stakeholders

When you start thinking about who the stakeholders in a given negotiation might be, let your imagination run wild. It is far better to start with too long a list of possible stakeholders than to discover later in the process that you left out a stakeholder whose interests could influence decisions made by any of the negotiating parties. You can always eliminate stakeholders after you have done sufficient research to conclude that they are tangential to the subject matter of the negotiation and will not have a meaningful interest in its outcome.

Create Your Interest Map*

When you have developed what you consider a realistic list of stakeholders, create an Interest Map. Write their names and descriptions—and underline them—on a large sheet of paper, flipchart, or whiteboard. The Interest Map works best when the various stakeholders are spread across the page, with "related" groups near each other. Leave as much space as you can under each stakeholder to allow room for noting his or her interests.

Be careful not to simply list the stakeholders from top to bottom. Don't risk imposing limits on yourself by trying to create a neat matrix. Interest Maps change as new thoughts occur to you or as you gain information from colleagues or other

*Copyright © 2001 by Steven P. Cohen. All rights reserved.

sources. Ultimately you will use the Interest Map to find connections among stakeholders and their interests in order to arrive at an agreement that responds to as many of those interests and stakeholders as possible. This is not to suggest that every negotiation will give everybody everything they want—a more realistic aim is to do the best you can, given the realities you face.

> **Interest Map** One of the best ways to test your assumptions is with an Interest Map. This fundamental preparation tool builds upon your use of assumptions to help develop a strategy for negotiating. As the accompanying illustration shows, an Interest Map begins with a list of the negotiating parties and other stakeholders.

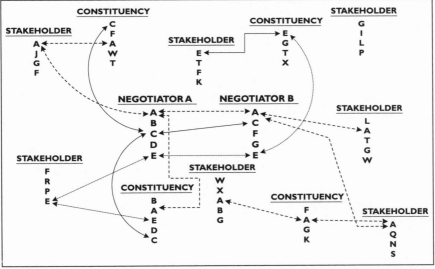

Figure 5-1. Interest Map, the letters listed under each of the parties represent their interests as we assume them to be

Record Your Assumptions About Stakeholders' Interests

When you have identified the stakeholders, the next step is to list your assumptions about their interests—particularly as they

Neatness May Not Count

It is important not to worry about the artistic integrity of the Interest Map's design, but rather to focus on creating a useful tool for discovering the interests of all parties and their constituencies. In addition, creating an Interest Map should give you space for drawing connections among interests that may be common or complementary. This will give you hints of possible areas where you can build agreement.

relate to the anticipated negotiation. You will gradually refine this initial list of interests as you learn more about the priorities of each party. Keep in mind that you hope to determine which one interest needs to be satisfied before the next one can be addressed. Remember that there are fundamental or primary interests as well as derivative or secondary ones. If the Interest Map does a good job of illustrating the assumed priorities of stakeholders' interests, it offers an excellent means to guide your information gathering before and during the negotiation process.

As is the case when you are first considering who should be considered a stakeholder, be creative and open-minded in trying to figure out the interests of stakeholders. Keep in mind that not everyone shares the same interests—what is important to you may have little significance to me. Remember that your constellation of stakeholders and their interests is initially a series of assumptions. Recognizing that fact makes you free to

Is It Only the Money?

We often assume that money is an interest that drives everyone, particularly in business. While this may be true, money can, and often does, represent different things to different parties. Money is a reflection of our value to others; it is a resource for savings; it is the means by which we measure and meet budgetary targets.

abandon assumptions that fail reality checks; after all they were only assumptions, not the rules of chemistry or elements of the Constitution.

What you are creating is a picture of the complex of stakeholders and interests that needs to be considered during the negotia-

Connecting the Interests of One Stakeholder
Part of the job in developing an Interest Map is to figure out how the interests of each stakeholder relate one to another. For example, if one of your interests is to make more money, perhaps a secondary interest is your concern about your reputation. It could well be that your reputation depends on how good a deal you make in this negotiation to enhance your general batting average. The kinds of deals you are assigned to pursue may well determine the likelihood of success. Going through a stakeholder's interests step-by-step and discovering how those interests connect to each other can help you reach wiser conclusions about your negotiation strategy and, as a consequence, reach more satisfactory results.

tion. Design the Interest Map so that it is relatively easy to draw lines connecting related interests of different stakeholders, especially among the negotiating parties and their immediate constituencies. Sometimes the connections of interests among related parties must take top priority; in other situations, finding connections among stakeholders on different sides of the issue is of greater importance.

Don't Go It Alone

Your first draft of your Interest Map is a product of your own understandings and assumptions about the situation. When you feel that it is a pretty good representation of how things are, confer with co-workers or other folks with whom you have some sort of relationship to get a reality check on your assumptions about their interests or the interests of other stakeholders. Bringing co-workers into the design of the Interest Map can be a major step in getting them to buy into the process and to develop

Buy-in Unless people feel that they have ownership in the negotiating process, they're not likely to feel a strong commitment to fulfill the terms of the resulting agreement. Make sure that people buy into the process as early as possible. Then check with them as often as makes sense under the circumstances to see if they still feel comfortable with the way things are going.

their confidence that you are taking their concerns into account as you go forward with the negotiation. Colleagues may also be able to provide you information about other stakeholders—the parties with whom you'll be negotiating, their constituents, and those who might be characterized as innocent members of the public who will be affected by the decision you and the other negotiators reach.

As your Interest Map is refined through work with your colleagues, look for other stakeholders in the overall deal who can inform you about their own interests and what they understand about the interests of other stakeholders as well as the parties to the actual negotiation. Your colleagues are only some of the outside stakeholders whose interest and information are valuable. Their information allows you to test and expand your initial assumptions.

Low-Cost Solutions

As you start the Interest Map process, keep in mind that you want to use it to find ways to respond to other stakeholders' interests at the least possible cost to yourself or your constituency. If the party being asked to disburse money as part of an agreement finds that the receiving party is more interested in an ego massage than in the sum offered, it may be possible to provide at least a portion of that ego massage by means other than cash. Sometimes we can demonstrate the value of our negotiating partner or massage his or her ego without using money at all. A key to the executive washroom or a good parking space may be worth more as an ego massage than several thousand dollars per year.

TRICKS OF THE TRADE

One Reason to Use an Interest Map

Information is the fundamental asset in negotiation. Your Interest Map offers you a mechanism for determining what information you need, what questions to ask, what assumptions to question, and what elements will be most helpful to you and other parties in reaching mutually satisfactory results through a good negotiation process.

Using an Interest Map gives you an opportunity to explore a panoply of creative ways to respond to stakeholders' interests. By looking at a variety of choices before you undertake the negotiation process, your solo work increases your range of alternatives—solutions or

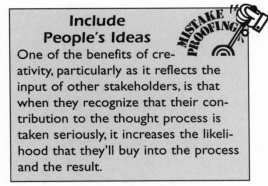

Include People's Ideas

One of the benefits of creativity, particularly as it reflects the input of other stakeholders, is that when they recognize that their contribution to the thought process is taken seriously, it increases the likelihood that they'll buy into the process and the result.

creative options you can utilize to respond to various parties' interests.

If you share the Interest Map process with colleagues or others, you are likely to find a further increase in the number of creative options. The creative options you find may well reduce the costs to you in terms of assets you have to trade to arrive at your goal. In addition, you may also discover that there are ways to meet your interests that might not have occurred to you if you were to rely only on spur-of-the-moment thinking.

A Timeline for Interest Mapping

The following steps describe the chronology of developing and using an Interest Map:

- Create a list of probable stakeholders.
- Check with colleagues for their suggestions of who should be added to—or subtracted from—the stakeholder list.
- On the largest writing surface available, write the names of the various stakeholders, grouped by their probable affinity with each other.
- Make a series of assumptions about the interests of the various stakeholders.
- List your assumptions about applicable interests under each stakeholder.
- Prioritize those interests based on your best guesstimates.

- Draw lines showing possible connections among stake-holders' interests.
- Use the Interest Map as a guide to the assumptions that need reality checks.
- Use the Interest Map to help you figure out what information you need in order to develop an agreement.
- Make a judgment call about whether to show the Interest Map to your constituents or to ask them questions about assumptions you have made. (In doing this, consider how people are likely to react before overloading them with information in which they may not be interested.)

Once agreement is reached, show your constituents how your Interest Map reflects the attention you and your negotiation partners paid to their interests.

How to Use Interest Maps

An Interest Map is a guide to help you figure out what information you need. It can help you ask questions that reveal other parties' interests as well as help determine your own interests and their relative priority. While Interest Maps are not a guaranteed way to solve all the issues that might arise in negotiation, they can help protect you from surprises.

Bringing about buy-in is a critical element when negotiation involves several stakeholders or constituencies. Working with your constituents to validate the assumptions you've made about their interests demonstrates you are paying attention to their interests. Asking questions of folks on the other side of the bargaining table is easier when you've thought of the questions in advance. Moreover, by asking questions and listening to the answers, you demonstrate

Non-Contract Contracts

Sometimes you can use an Interest Map as a non-contract contract. It may not be a legal document; however, if you take careful notes on the answers you receive and the agreements you reach, the Interest Map can form a skeleton upon which agreement documents are built.

Having All the Answers

Sometimes when a party thinks of every possible element that may be relevant to a given negotiation, he or she presents far too much information to his or her negotiation counterpart.

This sends the message that "I know everything, there's nothing for you to contribute to the decision." A salesperson who takes this approach runs the risk of unloading so much detail on a prospect that the potential purchaser is turned off by the hard sell. If someone has all the answers, you should question whether he or she really needs your contribution to the decision-making process.

---

that you are taking your counterparts seriously. Using their answers as building blocks for the proposals you make further demonstrates your commitment to responding to their concerns.

Using Your Interest Map in Negotiation

Your Interest Map can be utilized several ways in the negotiation process. Its primary purpose is to help you organize your thoughts ahead of time. It also works as a mechanism for gaining buy-in from other stakeholders. However, when you actually reach the negotiation session, it makes the most sense to keep the Interest Map as a private crib sheet or set of notes for your eyes (or your team's eyes) only.

If you approach your negotiation partner with your Interest Map and say, "I've thought of all the issues and here's how I see the situation," you're being positional and not giving your negotiation partner the opportunity to contribute to the decision-making process. No matter how much you have anticipated every likely scenario, a very real possibility remains that someone else may have a different viewpoint—and possibly a valid one at that.

Be Prepared for Hot Buttons

When interests or other issues are identified as hot button issues for one or more of the parties, the emotional temperature of the negotiation can rise. Keep in mind that a negotiation that focuses

> **⚠ CAUTION!**
>
> **Ruling Emotions**
>
> Although it can be appropriate to express emotions while negotiating, it is crucial to rule your emotions rather than let your emotions govern your behavior. If your preparation has included consideration of the emotional content of the issues that may arise during negotiation, you will have defused elements that might otherwise lead to the risk of explosion.

on emotional issues can be more challenging to bring to a mutually satisfactory conclusion. Focus on the issues about which you are negotiating rather than on the personalities of the parties. As you prepare your Interest Map, do as much research as you can on issues that might bring about emotional reactions.

This will help keep the negotiation process on a civilized level.

Donut Hole Interest Maps

Sometimes you find yourself negotiating in a situation where you or your negotiation partner—or both of you—are reluctant to reveal your own interests or let the other person know how those interests are prioritized. In these circumstances, creating a Donut Hole Interest Map can help.

The donut surrounding the hole is made up of the constituents of the negotiators as well as others who are stakeholders in the negotiation's outcome. It may well be that one of the negotiators attributes his or her interests to the boss: "If I come back with a deal like that, my boss will have my head!"

Be careful not to belittle yourself by telling your negotiation partner that you haven't got decision-making power. Say something like, "The deal holds a lot of promise, but I fail to see how it will benefit the end user of the product unless it includes the following specification."

Using the donut hole approach is a means for depersonalizing the issues that drive a negotiator's decisions. You can approach your negotiation partner by saying, "I don't know about you, but there are several constituencies who are concerned about the results I reach with you. Perhaps we ought to use a whiteboard or flipchart to get a sense of which constituencies are looking over our shoulders and what they want."

If your negotiation partner is willing to take this approach, you can develop an Interest Map together, which gives the negotiating parties a sense of which stakeholders and constituents and which interests of theirs are likely to be significant drivers of your decision making. If you focus on the constituencies—and not your own personal concerns—there could be a blank space in the middle of the Interest Map as the actual face-to-face negotiators are not describing their own interests but rather are focusing on those of other stakeholders. That blank space in the Interest Map can be thought of like the hole in a donut. If you and your negotiation partner become the "hole in the donut," you may develop a more collaborative approach to resolving the problems about which you need to reach agreement.

After the Negotiation

Remember that getting buy-in from your co-workers or other constituents is a crucial element in the long-term successful fulfillment of any agreement. When the negotiation process has reached its conclusion, it makes sense to go back to your colleagues and inform them about the following:

- How their interests have been addressed in the agreement you've reached.
- The relative value of their contributions to your development of your negotiation strategy.
- Feedback on the assumptions they had contributed or commented on as you assessed various stakeholder's interests and priorities in the planning process.

Acknowledging the contributions of your colleagues to your negotiation strategy is an important means of closing the loop of the preparation process. It should increase their commitment to fulfilling any obligations they have as part of the agreement and will certainly demonstrate that you have taken them and their ideas seriously.

Be Prepared

Satirist Tom Lehrer wrote a ditty many years ago, poking gentle fun at the slogan of the Boy Scouts: "Be Prepared. That's the Boy Scout Marching Song." In negotiation, being prepared is a critical means for increasing your competence and your confidence—and your capacity to respond calmly to unexpected issues. If you utilize Interest Maps whenever you have the time and opportunity to prepare, you enhance your capacity to negotiate effectively when preparation has not been possible. Developing good negotiating instincts is another form of inoculation; it can protect you from making many mistakes in the negotiation process and from agreeing to deals that you might regret afterward.

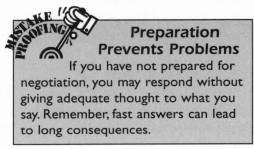

Preparation Prevents Problems

If you have not prepared for negotiation, you may respond without giving adequate thought to what you say. Remember, fast answers can lead to long consequences.

Manager's Checklist for Chapter 5

❑ Use assumptions about the interests of the stakeholders—including yourself—as you prepare for negotiation.

❑ Consider who the interested parties, the stakeholders, are. Who is likely to derive some sort of consequence as a result of the agreement between the negotiatiors?

❑ Create an Interest Map© that shows the stakeholders, your best assumptions of what their interests are, and how there could be connections between interests of different stakeholders, including the negotiating parties.

❑ Make assumptions about the priority of each stakeholder's interests. Which are fundamental or primary? Which are derivative or secondary? Do reality checks on these assumptions as the negotiation goes forward.

❑ Your colleagues may be a particularly valuable resource as you do reality checks on your assumptions about stake-holders' interests. Moreover, your colleagues' experience and knowledge can yield information that will help you develop your negotiation strategy.

❑ Time spent developing your Interest Map can aid achieving buy-in from your colleagues, protect you from surprises, and even make the negotiation process work more effi-ciently.

❑ A Donut Hole Interest Map can offer you and your negotia-tion counterpart(s) an opportunity to explore interests focusing on those of each of your constituents. It gives you a chance to bring up important issues without ascribing them to yourself.

❑ By underscoring your focus on interests, your Interest Map will help you avoid getting stuck on emotional hot buttons or cultural obstacles to developing a workable negotiation process and an agreement that works for the parties.

Communication: Key to Effective Negotiating

God gave us two ears and one mouth; we should use them in that ratio.

—old folk expression

Preparation Put to Use

Your preparation activity, particularly the Interest Map, outlines the assumptions you've made about who the stakeholders are and what you believe their interests are. If you've done a thorough job with the Interest Map, you have reached conclusions about the priorities of different stakeholders' interests as well as drawn lines to show possible connections among the interests of various parties. You have created the skeleton of what you assume will be the elements of a mutually agreeable result.

The Interest Map is not conclusive, however. It is merely a guide in your search for information during the negotiation process. What you need to find out now is whether the assumptions you have made about stakeholders, interests, priorities, and connections are accurate reflections of reality. Your Interest Map's job is to guide your information-gathering process to assist you in remembering what questions to ask when you sit down with the other parties. The questions you ask should be designed not only to validate or correct your assumptions but also to help you figure out the elements a wise agreement should contain.

What Moves During Negotiation?   Smart Managing

While the physical activity involved in negotiation may be limited to hand gestures, getting more comfortable in your chair, or writing notes, the process involves a tremendous amount of movement. Not only do BATNAs rise and fall in terms of their relative power, more significantly, information moves from party to party, influencing decisions. While it may sound like a cliché, the exchange of information is based entirely on how well the parties communicate.

One of the more frustrating elements of modern life is that we are surrounded by information. It is said that one day's edition of *The New York Times* contains more information than a well-educated European ran across in his whole life during the 14th century. Separating out the useful information from information that wastes our time is challenging enough; throwing away junk mail is a daily task for most Americans. In negotiation, separating the useful information from red herrings or ideas that might lead us astray is particularly important.

Communicating to Influence

We often mistake the ability to make a good presentation with the capacity to influence others. While speaking or writing well is certainly critical to making points clearly, it is not even half the battle in negotiation. Communication is a two- (or more) sided process. Good presentation is nothing without an audience to receive and process and respond to the presented material. While we can certainly influence others by presenting something to which they pay attention, the attention we pay to them helps us make the greater impact on the communication process.

In our information-overloaded society, people often feel ignored. Work is interrupted by phone calls, call waiting interrupts phone calls. When we try to reach customer service, we end up pushing buttons to get past the computer to a real human being. So many communications media compete for our attention that it seems as if everyone is treating us as their audience rather than as a source of interesting or relevant ideas. To negotiate well, we have to break away from that paradigm. Listening to other parties in the negotiation process can surprise them. When folks expect to be ignored, finding an interested audience can really break the ice.

Often when another party is making a point we find ourselves waiting for him to finish so that we can zap him with a brilliant comeback. When we do that, we are demonstrating that we are not interested in him or what he has been saying, but only in making our own point. Your brilliant remark may bring short-term satisfaction for you, but it brings about frustration for your listener.

Avoiding Clashes

People who do a good job of mediating disputes know that one of their most effective tools is to give the opposing parties opportunities to let off steam. This applies equally well in negotiation. After a person has vented his anger, he tends to relax physiologically with slower breathing and a slower heart rate. If attacked, however, the anger is likely to escalate and the level of civility among the people involved in the discussion is likely to decline.

When negotiating, it's important to remember that the main point of preparation is to figure out what sorts of information you need in order to reach a mutually agreeable conclusion. You already know the hard information available to you; your job is to learn what hard information is available to the other parties to the negotiation. You hope to find out whether your assumptions are correct. You can't get affirmation of the accuracy of your assumptions by presenting information, you can only do so by receiving it.

Active Listening

The cornerstone of the information exchange in negotiation is called active listening. There are several steps in the active listening process. While you shouldn't try to follow exactly the same stage directions every time you listen, consider each of the points below to determine which will bring the best results. As in most other elements of interest-based negotiation, your choice of how to listen and react to what you hear can vary with every interchange of information. The important thing is to be aware of the choices available to you and to make the right ones for the circumstances.

Pay Attention

In an ideal world, the negotiation could begin with your counterpart presenting you with all the information you need to validate or wipe out the assumptions upon which you've based your preparation. Whether others present an information-packed opening statement or merely a brief introduction to their viewpoint, pay close attention to your counterparts' initial remarks in order to learn which part of the information they present is relevant to the development of an agreement between you.

Control Yourself and Learn from Others

Your initial job is to learn what you can from the other parties. As this can take an enormous amount of self-control, it is perfectly appropriate to pat yourself on the back from time to time. Listen closely to what the other parties are saying. You should be trying to discern how the information they present might be relevant to elements in your Interest Map. In a sense, this calls for you to imitate a computer and perform multitasking: on the one hand, you are listening and absorbing information; on the other, you are figuring out what is going on in the negotiation process in terms of information exchange, overall strategy, and specific tactics.

Ask Questions

Sometimes you will find yourself facing parties who are not forthcoming with information. It is crucial to resist the tempta-

tion to jump in with all four feet and dazzle them with your brilliance. It is far wiser to ask questions, then listen closely for the information the answers contain, both in what is said and what is not said.

When another person is talking, listen for indications of his or her fundamental interests. Repeating a point frequently during conversation is a dead give-away that the point is very important. Pay close attention to the facial

TRICKS OF THE TRADE	**Ask Good Questions**

When you're negotiating, particularly during the information-gathering segment of the process, be careful not to ask questions that can be answered with a "yes" or "no." Ask open-ended questions, offering other parties the opportunity to express themselves in their own terms and offer details you would never get from the response to a multiple-choice question. Rather than asking, "Do you think the approach you propose will be good for our business?" inquire, "How do you think the approach you're suggesting will affect our business over the next six months?"

expressions and body language people use when they express a point. Keep an eye on whether they have organized their presentation and whether that organization—or lack thereof—reveals any details that can help you understand them better. Indications of emotion are also crucial ways whereby people

CAUTION!	**Listen to the Answers**

When you ask a question, listen closely to the response. If you don't very obviously pay attention, you will devalue the process in the mind of your counterpart and could miss information crucial to the ultimate result.

demonstrate the relative importance of a particular issue to themselves or to their constituents. And if a person keeps checking the time while he is talking, ask yourself whether it indicates that he faces a deadline. On the other hand, if folks start looking at their wristwatches while you are talking, be cognizant of the very different message they are sending.

While active listening means using your ears, supplement what your ears pick up by paying attention to what your other senses notice. Clearly this is easiest to accomplish in face-to-face negotiation, although it is possible to hear whether a person is smiling during a telephone conversation. Handwritten letters reveal a lot more than typed letters, although they are a rare commodity indeed. Expressions of emotion that you see in e-mail messages, such as :-), are poor substitutes for live communication. Sometimes, however, they take the sting out of potentially troublesome language. The more you pay attention to what and how other parties communicate, the greater the likelihood that your response will bring you closer to a mutually acceptable agreement.

Ultimately the parties with whom you are negotiating will finish their presentation. There are several ways you can respond.

The Power of Silence

As emphasized earlier, if another party's proposal is fundamentally unacceptable and your BATNA doesn't let you walk away from the negotiation, the best response can be silence. Put on a poker face and reveal nothing. Don't look angry, amused, or confused. Use the power of silence to communicate to the other party that he or she had better try again, because the proposal offered is not one to which you will react. People are threatened by silence; it is a powerful weapon. Use silence extremely carefully—it can be like killing a mosquito with a sledgehammer.

While silence requires considerable self-discipline on your part, it makes the recipient of the silent treatment think, "What did I say? Was I offensive? Did I demand too much or offer too little?" While you sit there, the other party has to undertake the heavy lifting, examining what he or she has said or done and trying to figure out a better way to make the point that will get you to respond with greater engagement. You are hoping that the party on the receiving end of your silence will attempt to reframe the proposal in a way you will find more appealing.

Do I Understand You Correctly?

More often, however, rather than responding with silence, respond with one or more questions:

- "Am I correct in understanding you to have said x and y and z?"
- "Could you explain what you meant when you said a and b but not c?"

One reason to check whether you have understood correctly is to let the other parties hear how their ideas sound coming from your mouth. They may say to themselves, "Good grief! That doesn't sound all that palatable. We had better rephrase our proposal to make it more appealing." Here again, you have not had to do any heavy lifting; your counterpart has to go to the trouble of restating his or her ideas.

The Obligation of Reciprocity

Another reason to check whether you have understood your counterpart correctly is to create an obligation of reciprocity. When you are confirming your understanding of what she's said, there is shock value to in your question. She thinks to herself, "Wow, he was listening to me!" When that happens, you have created an obligation of reciprocity. In effect you are saying, "I listened to you. When I respond to your proposal, you have a reciprocal obligation to listen to me."

Get on the Same Page

It is entirely possible that when you let another party know what you have understood her to say, she will realize that her point has not been properly understood. Getting the negotiating parties onto the same page is crucial if a workable agreement is to be reached. If one party is discussing one range of approaches and another party has an entirely different agenda, you may have a situation that one of my colleagues calls "Dueling Monologues." Talking at cross-purposes with little or no likelihood of finding common ground makes it difficult to reach meaningful, durable agreements. Unless the negotiators share an agenda in terms of discussing the same issues—even though their ideal outcomes may be different—they are not on the same page. Unless

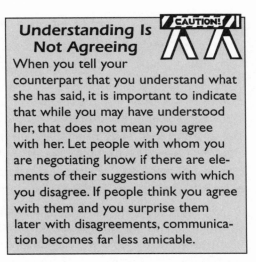

Understanding Is Not Agreeing

When you tell your counterpart that you understand what she has said, it is important to indicate that while you may have understood her, that does not mean you agree with her. Let people with whom you are negotiating know if there are elements of their suggestions with which you disagree. If people think you agree with them and you surprise them later with disagreements, communication becomes far less amicable.

negotiators are on the same page and committed to working on the same issues, a real agreement is unlikely.

Friendly Silence

The point where you and your counterpart agree that your understanding of what he has said is accurate is a perfectly good time to say, "Now that I understand you, I would like to think about your ideas before responding to them."

This is a very different use of silence than the poker-face approach. Here you are indicating that you have focused so much on the other party's points that you now need time to consider those points before you respond. Letting others know what you are doing during the negotiation process—acting transparently—can increase their comfort level in dealing with you.

After you have processed what they have said or proposed, the odds are that your reply will be more responsive. Show how their phrases or concepts have influenced what you say. This technique not only massages their egos but also increases the likelihood that you'll package your own thoughts in ways your counterparts will find more appealing than what you might have proposed if you were the first one to talk.

When Another Party Over-Communicates

One of the challenges to active listening is dealing with a party who never seems to stop talking. A story attributed to Mark Twain, probably apocryphal, relates that he once told his audience, "If you finish before I do, let me know." When your negotiating partner keeps raising point after point, you may want to interrupt him politely and say, "The points you are making are quite interesting. Just to make sure that we give each of them the appropriate amount of attention, perhaps we should discuss a few at a time rather than trying to deal with all of them at once."

If you are taking notes, you may be able to keep track of the points that have been raised. Even so, negotiation should be characterized by conversational give and take. If one party dominates the communication process, he or she is effectively "unleveling" the playing field.

Communicating with Difficult People

Often negotiation is made more difficult because one or more parties (1) doesn't want to negotiate or (2) takes a positional approach. If your BATNA gives you the flexibility to work with someone else, perhaps that approach is the best avenue. On the other hand, if you really need to engage in dialogue with a "tough guy," it is important not to delude yourself into thinking that your brilliant presentation will turn him around.

Asking questions demonstrates that you are interested as well as indicates that you take anoth-

TRICKS OF THE TRADE

Questions Rather than Assaults

It makes sense to ask questions. When someone says, "We have to connect the frammis to the jammis and that's that!" see what you can do to get a better sense of what interests lie behind that position. You can ask, "Could you describe the characteristics of the jammis that will make it work better with the frammis?" or "What sort of results will the ultimate combination you describe yield, and what will their effect be on the bottom line?"

er party's concerns seriously. Questioning is a far more convincing sign of respect than giving a lecture. In your Interest Map
research, look for personal details about the various stakeholders. Knowing that someone is a baseball fan, hates traveling, or
is allergic to dogs may not be a central issue in the negotiation
but can provide a way to break the ice. Part of what you want to
do is establish a climate of relatively easy conversation. An
agreeable climate can lead to developing the habit of agreeing
on "little" issues. Over the long term, the habit of agreement
may open the possibility of agreeing on issues that have a significant impact on the parties' interests.

Reframing

Sometimes a party to the negotiation presents an idea in a troublesome form. The language may be inoffensive to him while
you perceive it as unacceptable. It is also possible that his language is not a clear enough statement upon which to base
agreement. Under those circumstances, you need to reframe
the statement in language that is acceptable to more than just
one party. It could be as simple as saying, "Rather than indicating a and b and c, how would you feel if we modified the language to say b and a and c?"

When you attempt to reframe another party's language, you
must ask for their permission to change the language—or ask
whether there is agreement with the way you restate their point.
Think of how you would react if another party wanted to reor-
ganize one of your statements. Consider how to sell the idea of
reframing in the most palatable way. Suggest simplifying the
language or making a conscious effort to reflect joint concerns.
It could also be appropriate to say, "The proposal that's been
presented is not appealing in its current form. How can we
rephrase it to make it attractive to more parties?"

Asking an open-ended question keeps your negotiation
partner engaged in contributing to the process. A take-it-or-
leave-it response can close down the dialogue.

What Is Your Point?

If a critical focus of the negotiation process is to trade information back and forth in order to derive wise agreements, you need to keep your eyes on the prize. When setting up a conversation—as well as while it is going forward—keep asking yourself, "What is the point of this discussion?" Unless you have a purpose for the negotiation you've undertaken, it can be a waste of time for you and the other parties. Keeping focused on the information you need in order to reach a sensible result will help you behave more efficiently in the negotiation process.

Similarly, when another party to the negotiation seems to be headed in a direction opposite to making progress, asking him where he is heading can help you understand him better and improve communication between you. The question, "What is your point?" is not terribly polite; however, worded more diplomatically, such as "I find myself confused about where you are heading; could you please explain your objective more clearly?" could elicit information that overcomes obstacles to cooperative decision making.

Communicating Information

Remember that negotiation is not a one-sided activity. Trading information about needs, assets, prices, or other elements that can yield a workable result requires asking questions, active listening, and responding with ideas that use the information the parties have made available to each other for joint gains.

Introducing too much information can create a fog through which it is hard to travel. Look for points that are significant to yourself and to the other parties. Successful agreements are based on clarity of understanding—the fundamental purpose of communication. Laying all your cards on the table

Dumb Questions

As the saying goes, "There's no such thing as a dumb question. But there may be dumb answers." Don't give away information when it is contrary to your interest.

may seem like a "nice" thing to do, but presenting information other parties consider irrelevant can be viewed as a waste of everyone's time.

Manager's Checklist for Chapter 6

❑ Use your Interest Map to outline the information you need to acquire to check the accuracy of your assumptions about the interests of other parties and stakeholders.

❑ Look for information that helps you draw connections among interests and, in so doing, develop the elements of a wise agreement.

❑ Communication is a two-way street. You need to be able to do a good job of presenting your ideas in a way that will influence the decisions of your negotiation partners. It is even more important to hear their points so that your presentation is couched in terms that reflect your attention to your counterparts' ideas.

❑ Active listening involves several elements including paying attention, controlling yourself so that you can learn from others, asking open rather than yes-or-no questions, listening to the answers, understanding how to use the power of silence, making sure you are on the same page, and reinforcing the obligation of reciprocity.

❑ Questions are a more effective way to deal with difficult people than frontal assaults.

❑ Reframe troublesome or confusing statements to improve understanding and add substantive input to the discussion.

❑ Remember to keep asking yourself, "What is the point of this negotiation?" This reminder will help you stay focused on your interests, give you a sense of your BATNA in the negotiation, and should, as a consequence, keep you from wasting time.

❑ Laying all your cards on the table may confuse your negotiation partner with information she doesn't find relevant for her decision-making process.

Emotions: Dealing with Ourselves and Others

Stifle yourself!

—Archie Bunker to his wife Edith
in the TV sitcom "All in the Family"

Do Emotions Belong in Negotiation?

Many people think that negotiation has to be cold-bloodedly analytical and that the process will only work well by keeping emotions out of the picture. On the one hand, this is an unrealistic expectation that puts pressure on us to ignore or mask our feelings. On the other hand, emotions that get out of hand can create a tremendous obstacle to the likelihood of reaching agreement.

We can approach some negotiations without emotion, but other negotiations may involve hot button issues. Our egos may be on the line or the pressure we face from constituencies can place us under significant stress. It is crucial to remember that the same types of issues can face the other parties, even though we don't happen to feel emotional about any of their issues in the negotiation. To make the blanket statement that emotions don't belong in the negotiation process ignores the reality that negotiating is an activity conducted by human beings, not by machines.

Recognizing and Prioritizing Emotions

As you prepare for negotiation, try to figure out where there may be issues that could trigger an emotional response in you, in the other parties, or in other stakeholders. If you have an idea of where emotions might come into play, they are less likely to surprise you.

Understanding where your own emotions may come into play gives you the chance to consider whether, how, and why they should be expressed in the negotiation process. Choosing the time, place, and manner of how you are going to indicate joy, anger, or stress ahead of time is a crucial part of your preparation process. Planning that includes potential emotions can increase the likelihood that you will negotiate effectively.

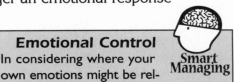

Emotional Control

In considering where your own emotions might be relevant, you take the first step in controlling your emotions rather than allowing your emotions to control you.

Planning Your Use of Emotions

Choreographing your use and expression of emotions can be an extremely effective tool. I will never forget a former boss of mine who was interviewed on television about a governmental action (actually, an inaction) that went against his interests. The interviewer asked him whether he was angry at the situation. His response was "Angry? You bet I'm angry!" Unfortunately there was a technical problem with the interview process, so the interviewer called a short halt and then began again. He asked my boss whether he was angry at the situation. His response, with the identical facial expression as the first time, was "Angry? You bet I'm angry!" My boss had decided ahead of time just how he would use his emotion to make a point. His planned use of his emotion made the interview very effective and it received considerable attention.

Surprise

If you are surprised by what another party says you need to consider, how you express your surprise will have an impact on the negotiation. Should you act insulted, threatened, or would it be better to sit back poker-faced and roll with the punches? What if someone offers you twice as much for a given item than the price for which you were aiming?

If you have done a good job of preparation, you have paid at least some attention to the wide range of issues that may arise during negotiation. While the specific details of another party's proposal may be different from what you had contemplated, raising the issue is not going to throw you for a loop. You will be able to place your counterpart's proposal in context, focusing on what it means rather than its emotional impact on you.

Coping with Surprise

Angus, a Scottish associate of a French-based management consulting firm, was working with Max, a very difficult American chief operating officer of a French division of a U.S. company. Among his problems, his French subordinates did not trust Max. Max asked Angus to meet with him to work on a variety of issues within the consulting contract. To his shock, on his arrival at the meeting, Angus found that Max was accompanied by nine of his French subordinates. Angus was so flustered at being faced with the unexpected crowd that he had a hard time focusing on the meeting's agenda. When you are faced with totally unexpected circumstances it is important to take time to catch your breath and analyze the situation. Ask yourself questions—and if it is appropriate, ask questions of other negotiators as well:

• What impact does this new situation have on my BATNA?
• How does it relate to my interests?
• Does what's happened offer me insights into the BATNA, interests, or significant issues faced by other stakeholders?
• What information is being communicated and what can I learn from it about my assumptions?
• Is the unexpected set of issues more significant as a factor in the negotiation process or as information with a direct bearing on the subject matter of the negotiation?

When the unexpected happens, reflect on your interests and on your BATNA. While the interests that you hope will be served by this negotiation may remain unchanged, things you learn during the process will inform you about possible changes in your BATNA. To negotiate effectively, you must ask how each idea raised in the negotiation is good for you—or goes contrary to your interests. Keeping track of your BATNA during the negotiation helps you decide whether you would be better off working with someone other than your counterpart.

What sort of impact does this unexpected idea or information have on the choices you can make? How can you deal with it in the context of this negotiation or your relationship with other parties in order to get closer to a wise agreement? Does it make more sense to pick up your BATNA and walk away? Or should you quit before you get behind?

Are You Negotiating to Solve a Problem or Have a Fight?

There's an old expression in negotiation, "Separate the people from the problem." In personal relationships, getting rid of one of the parties may be a solution, although most negotiations don't relate to finding a better date for the prom. Generally speaking, people get together to negotiate because each party finds it in his or her interest to derive some gain from the input another party has to offer. In business, and in many social circumstances, we face situations that are not peculiar to certain individuals but that relate to the interests of our companies, our neighborhood, or groups of friends.

In those more usual circumstances, the problem that needs to be solved will exist no matter who is charged with reaching resolution. It may be frustrating to negotiate with a person who is impolite, who behaves unfairly, or who just can't understand the ideas you are trying to communicate. But if we have no choice, we need to take steps to separate the person from the problem.

The underlying strategy is to find a way to give the problem a place of its own so that it doesn't reside in your body or in your negotiation partner. Simple approaches include the following:

- Put the problem on a whiteboard, a flipchart, or a pad of paper.
- It may be better to sit on the same side of the bargaining table rather than face off as adversaries with the bargaining table as the battleground between you.
- Use brainstorming techniques; throw imaginative solutions at the issue.
- Remember that no idea should be ignored initially; when you are brainstorming, you edit the ideas later.
- Consider your BATNA; if a person is really difficult, is there another way to solve the problem?

Utilize a Donut Hole Interest Map approach with your negotiation partner. Don't ask what they want—ask what the folks who look over their shoulders are expecting.

Your goal should be to create a collaborative process. Communicate a very simple idea to your counterpart: Each of us has been given responsibility to deal with this issue; let's act as a team, with the problem as our common adversary.

Confidence-Building Measures

Some people are self-confident when they approach a negotiation; others are insecure because they are negotiating with people they don't know. Many people are nervous about negotiating in general and suffer from stage fright—sometimes called *negotiation phobia*. Often negotiation phobia is based on the history of the relationship between the parties, which may make negotiation difficult. Some experienced business negotiators assume that the people with whom they are planning to negotiate have greater resources or more power than they themselves have. As a result, they approach the negotiation process anticipating the worst possible results.

When a rocky history or lack of self-confidence poses an obstacle, it makes sense to use the preliminary elements of the negotiation process as an opportunity to build mutual confidence.

Building Confidence Between States

Confidence-building measures can be significant in both major and minor negotiations. It is common in international diplomacy to lay the groundwork for formal negotiation with small gestures. As part of the process of increasing the chances that Cyprus and Turkey would be accepted for membership in the European Union, the leaders of the Greek and Turkish segments of the divided island of Cyprus met for dinner on a social basis before any substantive negotiations began.

Negotiating parties often begin with a few non-threatening steps that build confidence in each other and in the negotiation process. These steps may range from deciding when and where to meet, agreeing on which issues should be considered at a meeting, to discussing who will represent each party and why. Preparing the logistical elements of a negotiation allows the parties to get into the habit of agreeing with each other.

Don't walk into a negotiation with an immovable chip on your shoulder. The process may be difficult to start, but if you recognize the difficulty and look for opportunities to agree on small issues, you will be more likely to end up with a wise result.

Only One Person Can Get Angry at a Time

It can take a tremendous amount of self-control when another person is yelling at you to keep from interrupting him with some sort of retaliation. The danger is that what we may consider an equalizing retaliatory remark escalates the emotional heat. Your best interest is served by waiting your turn before you get angry. When another person is spouting off, focus on what a wonderful person you are to have so much self-control. "It's not my turn to be angry" is the statement of a person who is in charge of himself. If you are in charge of yourself, you can be a far more effective negotiator.

There is a very practical reason for allowing someone to express strong feelings. When people vent deeply felt emotions and have a chance to complete that venting without interruption, their heart rate and breathing rate tend to slow down. They relax. They've gotten their grievance off their chest and can

The Power of Silence

When someone has said something or behaved in a way you consider outrageous, perhaps the wisest response is to put on a poker face, betray no emotion, and sit there in silence. This response will most likely be quite unsettling to the party who has misbehaved. Silence can be sufficiently threatening that people may clean up their act without your having to say a word. If the person senses that he has offended you, he could want to improve the situation before you retaliate. However, be careful about using the power of silence. If you use it too often with a particular party, it can lose its effectiveness. Getting a reputation as someone who responds with poker-faced silence can also undercut the credibility of this approach. In some cultures, reacting with non-responsive silence is quite normal and should not be taken as a reflection on what you said.

take it easy, at least for a moment. They are far more likely to be open to listening to you.

Your reaction after someone has gone ballistic needs to be considered. If what that person has said has angered you, made no sense, or undercut your proposal, you need to consider how to respond. Does it make sense to retaliate in kind? Will retaliation provide some immediate gratification? Consider the practical consequences of retaliation.

Reacting to Emotional Outbursts

If another party's outburst has upset you, don't try to hide your feelings to the extent that it gnaws away at you. Maintain balance between simple acceptance and an equal and opposite response. Take a few moments to consider your choices. If a person's behavior dictates your behavior, that person controls you—you do not control yourself.

You may say, very calmly, "I listened to what you said, and if I understood you correctly, I've never heard a more insulting/ ridiculous/impractical proposal in my life. However, perhaps my understanding was flawed. It seems to me that if we want to solve the problem before us we ought to look more closely at what we each have to gain by working together in a cooperative manner. If we fail to reach agreement, how will each of us explain that to our bosses or other constituents?"

Your calm and reasoned response will clarify the communication and underscore the degree to which emotions should be significant in your negotiation.

> **The Problem Before Us**
>
> When you refer to the problem "before us" rather than the problem "between us," you are making it clear that the problem is shared and that the solution rests with the parties at the table. If you use the phrase "the problem between us," you are emphasizing the chasm of disagreement that separates the problem solvers from a solution.

De-escalation

Emotions that run high can deflect parties from their proper focus on the central issues of a negotiation. Thus you need to figure out how to manage the emotional content of the negotiation process. Remember that sometimes the expression of emotion can have a positive impact on the negotiation; letting parties know with a smile that you are pleased to be working with them is a very simple approach.

One of the most successful approaches to reducing unfriendliness, whether the unfriendly parties are expressing anger, disinterest, or an unwillingness to budge from their position, is to ask questions. Making it clear that you are interested in them increases the chances you will be able to open the door to serious discussion. When you ask questions, listen closely. Make it obvious that you are listening. Nod your head, raise your eyebrows, or lean forward with your chin on your hands to make it clear that you are paying attention. Focus on your response to counterparts whose emotions threaten to derail the negotiation. Your obvious interest in them and what they have to say should serve to communicate your intention to take them seriously. This active (or intensive) listening can defuse their fears that you may be hostile and at the same time reduce their feelings of hostility toward you.

> **⚠️CAUTION!**
> ## Managing Emotions
> While the attention you pay to other parties may not totally remove the emotional content they bring to the negotiation, it can serve to bring those emotions into context and down to a manageable level. Remember that emotions may be a necessary part of the negotiation process. If emotions dominate, however, the likelihood of reasoned agreement is substantially reduced.

Healing Relationships

Many negotiations take place between people whose relationship carries a heavy emotional content: married couples, parents and children, or close colleagues at work. Often past experience among the individuals has led to unsatisfactory processes in working out issues between them. Too frequently we get into a rut in the way we argue with people with whom we have a particularly close relationship.

If we focus on why something is important rather than allowing that particular issue to be the excuse for an emotional outburst, the cause of the dismay may be dissipated and the

> **TRICKS OF THE TRADE**
> ## Trading Accusations
> When spouses disagree, it often degenerates into a shouting match with the two people trading accusations: "You always say that!" and "Well, you always do that!" Years ago my wife used to accuse me of being a slob because I would leave a pile of my dirty clothing at the end of the bed at night rather than placing it in the laundry hamper. My response was to find some similar accusation to aim at her. As a consequence, we were stuck in a rut that never resolved the actual problem. Finally she told me that the pile of clothes made her nervous about tripping in the middle of the night. Instead of calling me names, she was describing her specific interest in changing the situation. By bringing the focus to her interest rather than to her annoyance with me, she changed the process we used in our disagreement. It was less about accusing me of being a slob and more about her interest in not tripping over an obstacle I placed in her path. Focusing on interests brought us out of the rut and healed a slightly troubled element of the relationship.

unfriendly style of problem solving may be rendered obsolete. This is not to say that the emotional content of the relationship should be ignored, rather that it should be placed in the proper context. We need to give more serious thought to what makes us angry, remembering that dealing with our interests is more rewarding than using what we perceive to be the interests of others to bring negative emotions into a relationship.

Dealing with Difficult People

Someone once defined a bureaucrat as a person whose entire self-image is built on his power to say "No." All of us run into people who refuse to consider alternatives to standard operating procedure, people who are threatened by change. If they are in a position to give or withhold permission for things we would like to do, they can drive us crazy. We often have to deal with people who have poor people skills, who make mountains out of molehills, whose inability to see other people's interests make us wish they would disappear in a puff of smoke.

Bullies

There are some folks who go beyond the description of difficult. Some people undertake negotiation as bullies; their objective is to demonstrate their own power and, perhaps, to cover up a

Make a Game of It

A woman in India sent me an e-mail asking for advice on how to deal with her live-in mother-in-law who had a habit of lying about nearly everything and who kept telling her son lies about his wife. My advice to the wife was to think of lying and nastiness as her mother-in-law's job. I advised her to wake up every morning with the expectation her mother-in-law would behave badly. Her role was to make a game of it: "How many lies will my mother-in-law tell today? Will she set a new record? I won't be satisfied until she's told at least 10 lies before noon." If you expect people to misbehave, every time they do so they are proving you right and you can add another point to your score.

weak self-image. In general, bullies may be described as people who are afraid of failure. If someone tries to act as the bully in a negotiation with you, the best approach to defuse the situation is to say, "From the looks of things, I'm afraid we may fail to reach agreement."

While you may not be threatened by failing to reach agreement with someone who is trying to push you around, a classic bully whose self-image may be weak could be threatened by the idea of failure. You will not only capture his or her attention, you will begin to open that person up to being more reasonable.

Expressing Emotions Is Not Bad Negotiating

The fundamental lesson of this chapter is that emotions are a legitimate part of negotiation. Emotions expressed by parties help their negotiation counterparts gain a better understanding of the interests that are involved and provide greater insights into parties' priorities. Emotions can be used to make points that rational arguments can't really express. If ...

- you think ahead about the issues that can bring your emotions to the surface,
- you consider what hot buttons may exist for your negotiation partner,
- you consider how that information can be used in developing and implementing an effective strategy,

the odds are the negotiation will be more effective.

If you let your emotions control you, you risk losing control as well as influence over the process. If you listen to the emotional content revealed by other parties, the information you derive can help lead you to a wiser result, a more durable agreement.

Manager's Checklist for Chapter 7

❏ You need to understand how emotions fit into a particular negotiation. They may help you learn more about what makes other parties tick, although you have to be careful

not to let emotions be an obstacle to focusing on interests
to achieve a wise agreement.

❏ Look for potential emotional issues during your preparation.
It will help you deal more intelligently with them should they
arise during the negotiation process. This includes planning
for your own use of emotions to underscore important points.

❏ Being open about hot button issues is not a sign of weakness. It is, however, a sign of weakness if you lose control of
your emotions.

❏ Plan your reaction to possible surprises before they arise.
This doesn't mean you'll know what surprises are going to
happen, only that you need to have a sense of the best use
of your negotiation style based on preparation, emotional
control, and effective communication.

❏ Separate the people from the problem. Is the negotiation
likely to yield a better agreement if you are working with
someone else or is it more realistic to treat your counterpart
as someone with whom you can gain an effective result by
collaborative efforts? Remember the problem is "before" us
rather than "between" us.

❏ Confidence-building measures can help overcome negotiation phobia by giving the parties practice reaching agreement on nonthreatening issues.

❏ Consider the practical consequences of emotional retaliation. Will it move things forward or backward? A response of
silence can be more powerful than a shouting match.

❏ Ask questions to reduce hostility.

❏ When people persist in being difficult, make their misbehav-
ior a game that amuses you rather than an annoyance that
rankles you.

Dealing with Annoyance and Leveling the Playing Field

Cheat me once, shame on you.
Cheat me twice, shame on me.

—old folk saying

Myths

Through the centuries and from culture to culture, myths have become accepted as the conventional wisdom to describe how to succeed at negotiation, including which elements of human interaction are open for negotiation and which are not. Some people believe that negotiation is only used to resolve conflicts. Others think it is a business tool, only used in sales, purchasing, salary negotiations, or other financial situations. When you say the word "negotiation," some people think you're referring to what goes on between labor unions and business management. One of the toughest myths people face in negotiating is the belief that the negotiation process has to be treated as an adversarial interaction and that when it comes to strategies and tactics, anything goes.

The reality is that whenever people interact to reach a decision or agreement, some form of negotiation is taking place. There are different approaches to the negotiating process and negotiators can—and should—choose the one that makes the most sense under the circumstances. Negotiation is definitely *not* a one-size-fits-all process. To do a good job you have to be creative, analytical, and flexible. You also need to keep your eyes and ears open to learn how others are approaching the negotiating process.

Let's look at some of the myths or games you might encounter in different negotiating situations:

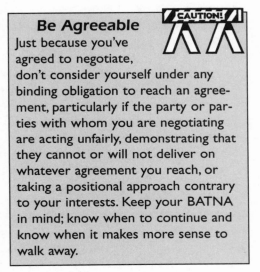

Be Agreeable

Just because you've agreed to negotiate, don't consider yourself under any binding obligation to reach an agreement, particularly if the party or parties with whom you are negotiating are acting unfairly, demonstrating that they cannot or will not deliver on whatever agreement you reach, or taking a positional approach contrary to your interests. Keep your BATNA in mind; know when to continue and know when it makes more sense to walk away.

The First Person to Name a Price Loses

Some people believe that they should not name a price in negotiation but instead react to what the other person suggests. If every negotiator followed this advice, no one would ever make a deal or reach an agreement. If there is a financial element that has to be included in the ultimate agreement, be extremely careful to figure out the price that goes furthest toward serving your interests. With a reasonably clear understanding of your financial objective, whether it is a matter of how much you are willing to pay or the appropriate selling price, you are in better shape when the money aspect of the deal arises and you can name a price you believe is appropriate.

Only Tough Negotiators Win

Here's another game some people feel they need to play when they negotiate. Negotiations based on crushing the opposition through persistent use of nasty behavior are likely to leave at

Salary Negotiation

Let's say you're a new college graduate looking for your first job. As you proceed, you need to understand the market for people in the job you hope to acquire, including salary range. Another important part of your preparation should include figuring out how your interests will be served by a range of possible elements in the compensation package: salary, benefits, career ladder, and so on. How much will you need for food, clothing, and shelter? Decide on a minimum figure. If the person interviewing you asks how much you want to be paid, offer a range that begins slightly above your minimum. For example, if you've concluded $30,000 per year is the appropriate starting salary, suggest you are looking for something in the "low to mid-thirties." Give your interviewer a chance to feel good if she offers, say, $31,000. This mean that she has taken the opportunity to reduce the offer from the upper end of the range you proposed. And you still end up where you want to be.

least one of the parties feeling resentful and looking for ways to avoid fulfilling the agreement. This is the "winning by intimidation" approach. While it can be a useful strategic move to let your negotiation partner know that you've got a strong BATNA, being loud and assertive about any aspect of the negotiation does not add credibility to your position. When you are calm and clear in your mind that you have attractive alternatives, the self-confidence you exhibit is far more believable than all the bluster in the world. People who take a harsh approach in their negotiating behavior are often exhibiting a lack of self-confidence that is sometimes based on an inability to deliver or a lack of authority to make a decision. Sometimes their approach is based on the fact that what they have to deliver is not as valuable as they are trying to force you to believe.

Putting the Other Party on the Defensive Through Interrogation

Asking questions is a critical element of negotiation. If you're looking for information and don't ask questions, you are not likely to find out what you need to know. Sometimes you'll encounter people who don't want to volunteer information. They know the information they're looking for—their tactic is to barrage you with questions. If this happens to you, think hard before responding. Try to figure out how your response will serve *your* interests. If you are confused by another party's question, there's nothing wrong with responding with a question, "Why are you asking me that?"

Their answer may help you gain insight into their interests, their BATNA, and, often, what it will take to sell them on the approach that most appeals to you. When individuals ask a lot of questions but are hesitant to answer your questions, those persons may have something to hide about their BATNA and/or the value of their offer.

Responding to Macho Negotiation Tactics

Some people who have negotiated frequently have developed long lists of ploys and tactics they believe are appropriate in facilitating negotiation and getting what they want from the other party. While it is certainly possible to memorize a negotiator's playbook, the real challenge you face is looking at the circumstances and paying attention to your gut feeling about what's going on. Keep asking yourself, "Is this a tactic she is attempting to use on me?" Ask yourself how the other person's behavior and attitude make you feel. Sometimes negotiators take a calculated approach, choosing to implement their strategy using a preplanned bag of tricks.

Good Cop/Bad Cop

One of the tricks negotiators sometimes try to use is the good cop/bad cop routine in which one of your counterparts purposefully plays the tough guy while his teammate utilizes charm on you. If you are getting conflicting signals from a negotiating team, let them know that you are not an idiot, that you can tell what is going on. Be careful not to accuse the other team of bad manners. Instead say something like "I feel as if I am being good cop/bad copped in this negotiation and it is not bringing me any closer to agreement." An alternative approach is to say, " Bill, Ted, it sounds like I'm getting mixed messages from you. Do you think it would help if I left you alone for five minutes so you can reach agreement among yourselves?"

Other times, the negotiation process presents opportunities to take advantage of the situation. You know whether you feel good about how the process is going. Expressing your feelings in a way that reminds the other parties that you are paying attention and responding to what you see or hear can effectively defuse games negotiators try to play.

Taking notes demonstrates that you are keeping a record of what is going on. The questions you ask that home in on the process, "Why did you ask me that question?" or your statements about the process, "I feel uncomfortable seated here with the sun in my eyes," will tell the other negotiators you are paying attention to what is happening. If you keep your BATNA in mind, it gives you a sense whether you are better off heading in another direction when you are not comfortable with the other parties' approaches to negotiation. If you feel there's a hidden agenda at work, be prepared to say something like "I have this feeling there are important issues that are not being discussed. Is there more I should know about what is driving your thought process?"

Negotiating according to a playbook or following a preset process can potentially put one of the negotiating parties at a disadvantage as it excludes the flexibility to conclude successfully. After all, another party with whom you are trying to reach agreement may well have good ideas for serving your interest. Blocking out his or her contributions because something else he or she has done has annoyed you means you are limiting the choices available for reaching results that might turn out better than if you

---

TRICKS OF THE TRADE

Self-Assertion Increases Your Credibility

When you spot someone trying to take advantage of you by using negotiation tricks—or if your gut tells you things aren't being handled fairly—then is the time to assert yourself. While it may initially feel embarrassing to complain about something as trifling as the sun in your eyes, your assertion of your awareness of a trick or your discomfort with an element of the process early on will establish your credibility as an intelligent person on whom tricks or unfairness will not work.

had worked alone. Remember, the reason for negotiating in the first place is to derive the benefit of contributions of ideas or other assets from other parties that you may not have thought of or be able to deliver on your own.

Psychological Games

Years ago, during my career as a Washington lobbyist, I met with a lobbyist from a labor union to try to forge a coalition on a particular issue. While her office was large and sumptuously furnished, the most striking thing about the setting was the seat of the chair behind her desk—it was substantially higher than any other seat in the room. As a consequence, she was guaranteed to be in a position to look down on anyone but a giant.

Looking up at the person with whom you are negotiating can create a psychological advantage for that person by making it appear that he or she is the one in control of the situation. The lesson I learned was never to meet again in her office. If I had used my sense of humor in that first meeting, I could have sat on a pile of cushions from her sofa to level the playing field. Or perhaps I should have put my feet on the sofa cushions and sat on the sofa back, thus capturing higher ground.

Asserting that you understand what is going on when people may be trying to take advantage of you not only reminds them that you deserve to be treated with respect, it also increases your credibility as a negotiator. Reacting by leveling accusations at the other party, however, can turn the negotiation

---

Let Them Know You Know

Tricks of the Trade

If other negotiators in a multiparty negotiation try to freeze you out while their allies are making a side deal with other parties, let them know that you understand what's going on. You can say, "You know, I have this feeling that something is going on behind my back." Calling attention to your capacity to analyze the process reminds the negotiators that they have an obligation to treat you with respect. If someone attempts to put one over on you and you say nothing about it, you are giving a cue that the person can continue with the behavior and perhaps bulldoze you on the most important matters in the negotiation.

into a shouting match. When you assert your right to be treated with respect in a courteous way, you help establish a sound foundation for productively moving the negotiation forward.

Giving or Taking Offense

One of the most challenging things in negotiation is that, even with people you know reasonably well, you may not know what their hot buttons are. As most people do not want to offend others, we need to distinguish between giving offense and offering constructive criticism. Your negotiations do not take place in a vacuum. If what you say or do gets other parties annoyed, their annoyance may override their focus on their interests and this can block the progress of the negotiation. While you have to be careful not to offend people without reason, you should be straightforward about troublesome things that impinge on your relationship or your capacity to work together to reach agreement.

It's important not to fall into the trap of going out of your

I Wanted to Be a Nice Guy

Several years ago, after my wife repainted our bedroom we had to move into the guest room while the paint dried. To our dismay, my wife and I discovered the guest bed was probably the worst bed in North America. We had no choice but to replace it. During that process, I called one of my oldest friends who had been a frequent houseguest. "Terry," I asked, "how would you describe the bed in our guest room?" He responded, "Steve, that may be the worst bed I've ever had to sleep on." As a consequence of his desire not to offend, he and other houseguests had suffered an untold number of bad nights' sleep. No one gained from his being a nice guy—neither our guests who had to endure the bed nor ourselves who were inadvertently treating our guests poorly. A couple of years later I was the guest in a friend's flat in London while he was away for an extended period. The place was missing all kinds of necessities—including toilet paper. I called him and suggested he have a word with the person responsible for maintenance. I was doing him (and his future guests) a favor by calling attention to the possibility that the maintenance person was taking unfair advantage of my friend.

way to be inoffensive; if you go too far in that direction, you may fail to provoke imagination or creativity in your negotiation partners or in yourself. Like emotions, calculated provocations can contribute significantly to the forward progress of joint decision making. On the other hand, don't forget to be especially attentive to the response your provocation yields; if the person at whom it is aimed gets angry, apologize quickly and explain what you were doing. This sort of transparency in the negotiation process increases the likelihood that parties will trust each other and ultimately arrive at a wise agreement.

Controlling the Board

As stated earlier, information is the fundamental asset of negotiation. Control of the means of communicating that information can have a significant impact on the outcome of a negotiation process. If one person is taking notes for all the negotiating parties, the note-taker may change a word here or there

---

Gratuitous Offensiveness

CAUTION!

Gratuitous offensiveness is more than bad manners; it is likely to turn off the offended parties and reduce the likelihood that a negotiation will be successful. Some people need to be very close when they talk; others need lots of space. If someone keeps backing away from you, ask him whether he would be comfortable with more space between you. It may be hard for him to say it, but perhaps you shouldn't have had an onion sandwich before starting the conversation. As you cannot always know what will offend another person, it could be practical, as well as polite, to insert into the early part of a negotiation a statement like this: "We don't know each other very well. If I should say or do something you find even mildly offensive, please let me know. I have no desire to offend you, and your advice will be appreciated."

Most people are like my friend Terry; they are not likely to give you lessons in what they consider good behavior. Nonetheless, by indicating that you have no intent to give offense, you demonstrate the good faith of your intentions. When someone does tell you that a particular behavior or sort of language is not appropriate, thank him or her. They have done you a real favor.

and, in so doing, influence the details of the ultimate agreement. You need to decide how the information discussed will be recorded and by whom. If ideas are listed on a whiteboard or flipchart, does only one party have access or can anyone record thoughts on that medium, which, after all, is the common property of the negotiators?

As part of your preparation, think about how to get ideas on the table. Should you present your entire proposal all at once? In many situations, it makes more sense to go step by step, measuring other parties' responses along the way. Think about how effective it is to let others present their ideas first. The more you can learn from them, the greater the likelihood that your response will reflect their ideas and, as a result, be more attractive to them.

Physical Set-Up

Consider how the physical set-up of a negotiation can influence the process. If you and the other parties in the negotiation are sitting on opposite sides of a table or desk, that piece of furniture can symbolize a divide between you. One way to overcome that divide is to arrange the seating so that parties representing different points of view are next to each other. This works particularly well as the issues to be resolved have a "home" of their own—a pad of paper, flipchart, or other recording medium equally accessible to everyone. If anyone has to read the notes upside down, that person is at a disadvantage.

Sometimes choosing the venue can have important symbolic value. If I come to a place of your choosing, there's a degree of reciprocity that I expect from you. A party who travels to another's turf gives up the home court advantage and deserves some sort of consideration for taking that step.

Building Confidence in Your Counterpart

Part of the venue choice process is a reflection of the relationship among the parties. If the parties have a longstanding, mutually respectful relationship, setting the time and place for negotiation should be reasonably simple and trouble-free. On the other hand, when the negotiating parties lack confidence in one another, time and place choices can be quite significant. By traveling to your turf, I send a signal that I want to do you the honor of going to you rather than expecting you to come to me. In some cultures where providing hospitality is an important norm, not meeting at a location chosen by the home team may cause them to lose face before you've even opened your mouth on substantive matters.

> **Key Term**
>
> **Confidence-building gesture** This is an action one of the parties to the negotiation takes to enhance trust in the other party. Such gestures suggest sensitivity to and respect for the other party's position and what he or she brings of value to the table. Working together ahead of the formal negotiation on logistical issues is one way the parties can build mutual confidence.

Confidence-building measures are attempts by negotiation counterparts to give other parties an opportunity to derive comfort from the situation and to develop the belief that negotiation may very well yield a good result. Arriving on time, dressing appropriately, using proper forms of address, avoiding off-color

> **For Example**
>
> ### The Shape of the Table
>
> Perhaps the most famous example of confidence building in recent history occurred as the Paris peace talks between North Vietnam and the United States were getting under way in the early 1970s. Each side had a profound distrust of the other. For the first 18 months of the process, diplomats from the United States and North Vietnam negotiated over the shape of the bargaining table. Nothing of substance was decided during that period; however, the process of reaching agreement on the bargaining table's shape gave the negotiators from both sides confidence that they could fashion a substantive agreement that would bring an end to the war. In business, confidence-building measures can be as simple as having coffee together, agreeing on the agenda of a meeting ahead of time, or fast follow-through on promises made during the negotiation that can be delivered before the final agreement is concluded.

language or jokes, and similar displays of sensitivity can go a long way toward increasing the mutual confidence between parties. Conversational small talk among parties before formal negotiation begins is one step toward building mutual confidence. Finding things you have in common can open many negotiating doors.

I Understand You, But That Doesn't Mean I Agree with You

We have examined the importance of clear communication leading to understanding as one of the fundamental elements of effective negotiation. Unless parties are on the same page—discussing issues that are understood the same way by everyone involved—the agreement can end up based on a misunderstanding. In that case, one or more parties may be reluctant to fulfill the agreement because it is not what they thought it was. Be careful not to take another party's apparent understanding of your point to mean that they have accepted it as part of an agreement.

One of the critical purposes of active listening is to bring the parties to the same page in terms of understanding one another. This is why it is so important to ask, "Have I understood you correctly to say a, b, and c?"

It is equally critical to be very clear that your understanding does not necessarily mean agreement. Remember to follow up with "Now that we're clear that I have understood you accurately, please don't assume that my understanding of your point means I agree with

⚠️ CAUTION!
Don't Get Fooled by a Smile
Sometimes negotiators give others the impression that they agree by indicating "I hear where you're coming from." As the point is not addressed again, one party may think his idea has been accepted and give unwarranted concessions on other issues under the false impression that the first issue has gone his way. Don't let a smile or a nod give you the wrong impression; if another party nods as you say something, ask, "Does that mean you agree with me?"

it. As I will explain, there are some elements of your approach with which I disagree."

When you make this point, you are setting out the agenda of what remains to be negotiated.

Expectations

While many elements covered in negotiation have nothing to do with money, financial issues tend to be a factor in virtually every negotiation, particularly in business. In order to do the best possible job of serving your interest, your preparation should include a focus on price issues. Keep in mind that while money may not be a central concern of all negotiators, the interests that will drive their decision making do include aspirations or expectations that may still be quantifiable; for example, in a situation where a divorcing couple is concerned with who gets how much time with the children. The points that are made in this paragraph may be about money, but negotiators can use the same sort of reasoning to help in a situation where nonfinancial issues are the focus of the bargaining.

As you prepare to negotiate, develop a realistic set of aspirations and expectations. Whether you are buying a house, 10,000 widgets, or negotiating a salary, your preparation must include gathering information about the market. Look at what either you or the company you represent can afford. If you're negotiating for a salary, for example, figure out how much you need to make to live in a given community, whether you need resources to pay back student loans, and so on. Consider how the price that is paid—or the salary you receive—will reflect on your competence, affect your reputation, and/or impact your ego. Develop a clear sense of your bottom line.

Once you have established a bottom line, choose how best to use the negotiation process to assure you will do no worse than that. It makes excellent sense to consider the situation of your counterpart; what can you learn about his or her financial flexibility? How can you make certain that this person will buy into a result that gets you where you want to go? Is there a

---

Fear of Offering Too Little

When a married couple I know found a house they just had to buy, the asking price was $250,000. Inspecting the house, they noticed that there was hardly any furniture and that the heating was set to a very low temperature—indications that no one was living in the house. The couple also knew that mortgage interest rates were on the high side. Through research, they also learned the house had been on the market for more than a year and that the asking price had already dropped by $100,000. The couple looked at their own resources and estimated how much it would cost to repaint the house and do some modifications to make it fit their needs.

They concluded that the most they could pay to purchase the house was $190,000. Although they were fearful that offering so much less than the asking price might offend the seller, they realized that they would never get the house without making an offer. In a calculated gamble, their opening offer was $190,000. The sellers grumbled a little bit, but did not ask for a higher offer; they accepted the $190,000. About a year after buying the house, the couple learned that when it had been on the market for $350,000, a potential buyer had considered offering $275,000 but decided not to for fear of insulting the sellers.

---

chance the other party will be offended if you ask for too much or offer too little?

Make offers that are realistic for *you*, that won't break your bank. You never know whether your counterpart will accept your offer straight out, say it is not the price they want and make a counteroffer, or walk away from the deal. If there is a counteroffer, you can decide how to respond depending on your resources and priorities. If your counterpart has walked away and you have the capacity to change your proposal, consider how to do it in a way that saves face for both of you. The attention you pay to the psychological issues can help rescue a deal that once looked doomed.

High-Ball/Low-Ball

Some negotiators make a conscious choice to begin with what seems like an outrageously high or low proposal. This approach

---

You Are Not Likely to Get More than You Expect

One of the mistakes people make during preparation is to overdo their focus on objections the other negotiating parties may raise. If you lower your expectations before negotiations begin, you are virtually certain not to reach optimal results. While it is wise to consider other parties' possible objections or contrary interests, they should not limit your hopes before negotiations start. Keep focused on your interests (while respecting the interests of others) and you are less likely to give things away before you are asked to do so during the bargaining process.

---

sets the tone for future rounds of bargaining. It is also an excellent way of testing the waters. Observing your counterpart's response can give you significant information about what you can expect as the negotiation goes forward.

The other side of the high-ball/low-ball approach is that a salesperson may use it in a sales negotiation to convince someone to do business with her company rather than with competitors. In its ugliest form, this approach can degenerate into a bait-and-switch situation where potential customers are drawn in by a price substantially more attractive than what is normal for the market. After being lured into the negotiation, factors are introduced to convince customers that they would be better off buying another, more expensive product, or features are added to the product that had been offered at a below-market price that will increase its profitability to the seller.

> **Key Term**
>
> **High-ball/low-ball** The initial posture in a negotiation where one of the parties asks for either everything he or she could possibly imagine from the other party or offers the bare minimum for what the other party has to offer. It can be a useful strategy but can also insult the other person and start the discussions off on the wrong foot. If you ask for a lot—or offer a little—think of the proposal as opening the door to negotiation rather than as a position that reduces your flexibility.

> **⚠ CAUTION!**
>
> ### Don't Let Yourself Be Fooled
>
> If someone proposes a price that strikes you as unrealistically low—or high—it probably is. Keep your focus on the price range that is neither low nor high but rather is *right*. This may remind you of the spin some companies use when they lay off employees, announcing they are "right-sizing" rather than "downsizing." If you have done a thorough job of preparing, you have a good idea of the right price for the commodity about which you are negotiating. If you keep the right price in mind, you won't be fooled by a negotiator who hopes to lure you in by giving you the impression he is offering a far more attractive deal than you're likely to find in the real world.

Early Wins Can Be Traded Away Later

As you prepare for negotiation, consider the priorities of your interests and objectives. There may be issues that arise in the negotiation process that are not terribly important to you, yet they may offer you the opportunity to create value for the other party. If you take each issue seriously, perhaps you will be able to convince your counterpart to see things your way on an issue you don't really care too much about. If you have worked hard for a result, you encourage your negotiation partners to feel that their concession on that point has been important to you. Later in the negotiation when an issue of higher priority to you arises, you may want to trade away the earlier gain in exchange for getting what you want on the higher-priority issue. Your efforts to get the favorable result in the earlier issue will increase its value when you offer to trade it away to your negotiating partner when the later, more important issue arises.

Level Playing Field

It is unrealistic to expect that all negotiations will take place on a level playing field. Negotiators have different BATNAs; the quality of their preparation will vary; and their innate or learned negotiation skills will generally be different. To negotiate successfully, focus on your interests and pay attention to your gut feeling. As a result, an uneven playing field can be less of an obstacle to reaching a wise agreement.

Manager's Checklist for Chapter 8

❏ Many myths surround negotiation. By focusing on interests and a fair process, the obstacles the myths may present can become less significant in blocking progress. Negotiation is not a one-size-fits-all formula for reaching agreement.

❏ Avoid letting these myths and behaviors confuse your negotiation process:

- The first person to name a price loses. Offer a price range that works for you.
- Only tough negotiators win. Quiet confidence is more convincing.
- Putting the other party on the defensive through interrogation. Think of how your response will support your interests.
- Responding to macho negotiation tactics. Assert your own intelligence and competence by asking yourself and your counterparts why they're using a particular tactic.

❏ When another party is using tactics that make you feel uncomfortable, they may not get the point unless you let them know. Don't make accusations; that raises their defensiveness. Simply talk about how you feel. Then they should get the point.

❏ Don't let offensive words or actions from other negotiators—or you—derail progress. However, don't fail to let others know what is bothering you; don't assume they have an interest in offending you.

❏ Controlling the board or the place where information is being recorded can have a significant impact on the process.

❏ Try to make sure you are on the same page with other parties. Unless you share an understanding of what you're discussing, you may be agreeing to two or more different interpretations of a contract.

❑ The lower your aspirations, the less you are likely to gain from your negotiations. Understand your resources well enough to avoid making unrealistic offers.

❑ Focusing on your interests and BATNA can help level a negotiation's uneven playing field.

Globalism Starts at Home: Cross-Cultural Issues

If a man says something, and his wife is not there, is he still wrong?

—old vaudeville joke

Nationality Is Not the Only Difference

With the growth of globalization and multinational businesses, people often think that knowing how to negotiate with different sorts of folks starts and ends with issues of cultural pluralism based on nationality. Indeed there are negotiation styles associated with people from certain countries. You must be cognizant of taboos, such as not showing the bottom of your shoe in Southeast Asia or touching another person with your left hand in many parts of the world. However, even within families and corporations you find tribes with differing mindsets. In a large enough business, you can find considerable differences in interests as well as in negotiation style between such groups as the purchasing department and sales force, designers and people involved in the manufacturing process, human resources professionals and bean counters.

125

You've Got to Be Kidding!

Imagine that you have just made a sale, agreeing to deliver 10,000 widgets in three weeks to your customer at a price of 32¢ per unit. If you haven't checked with your manufacturing division, when you let them know you've committed to deliver 10,000 units in three weeks they may say, "You've got to be kidding!" The same response may be forthcoming from elements of your company concerned about pricing. You need to get your colleagues from different tribes to buy into the approach you plan to take before negotiating a commitment to customers with which they do not agree.

In order to negotiate effectively with outsiders, whether they are from across the industrial park or from across the world, you must first conduct successful internal negotiations. Unless your team is in fundamental agreement, you run the risk of alienating them if you present them with a *fait accompli* resulting from external negotiations.

Internal Negotiation

Think back to the Chapter 5 discussion of Interest Mapping that discusses the need to utilize the contributions colleagues can make to the development and refinement of your Interest Map before negotiations. By bringing your co-workers into the preparation process, you give them the opportunity to feel ownership of the process and, as well, ownership of the result of your external negotiations. If you bring co-workers into the preparation process often enough, ultimately you will be able to develop a shorthand for collaborative decision making that should speed up the process.

Decision-making processes within families or among groups of friends are good examples of how internal negotiations should work. While individual characteristics or tastes may vary considerably (particularly among a family's generations), the negotiation process itself becomes a mechanism for bringing the group together. Family members or friends come to accept—or at least expect—the peculiarities of other members of the group. As a result, their collective decision-making process becomes increasingly smooth.

No matter how well you know someone, there is always the possibility of surprise. People who have been married for many years need to continue paying attention to the subtle messages their spouses send. While wives often describe their husbands as works in progress, the fact is that no one is the same person all their lives. Staying open to the unexpected in long-term relationships is at least as important as paying close attention to what a new business associate is telling you about herself.

Sometimes relationships between parents and teenagers, for example, can be challenging. Parents and kids rarely share tastes in terms of clothing, music, or the desired hour for waking up in the morning. In these instances, differences need to be ranked at a lower priority than the relationship itself. Rather than trying to win your negotiation with a teenager on his or her curfew, a wise parent should use the fact that there is some form of real communication as a mechanism for striving toward an adult relationship that will work when the children have left the nest.

Internal negotiation is particularly important as business organizations merge, participate in joint ventures, or otherwise create the need for people from diverse corporate cultures to work together. Organizations tend to have standard operating procedures. Subtle conflicts of language—job titles, for

Tribalism

The variety of tribes within a company can be astounding. In healthcare, for example, cardiac surgeons have a reputation for arrogance while psychologists are thought to be easy to push around. Hospital administrators and the various insurance companies and government agencies often appear to be driven entirely by the bottom line. Nurses have to mediate among different medical services, opposing sides of a patient's family, and staff responsible for food or logistical services. Each of these groups is a tribe that somehow has to work together with the others in order to yield a good outcome for the consumers of healthcare. Internal negotiation is crucial to bring about successful working relationships.

example, or differing mission statements—can become obstacles to effective collaboration. A high percentage of major mergers fail; all too often ego clashes, whether corporate or personal, are the root cause of such failures. Effective internal negotiation focused on enhancing understanding and communication can increase the likelihood of successful cooperative activity.

Bringing Tribes Together

When you're given responsibility for a task, you need to figure out your BATNA: the resources you have under your control—or influence—to achieve your objectives. Determine what resources exist within your organization or within a related company with which you could work in order to get closer to achieving your objectives. If the in-house resources originate from different tribes, you need to develop a better understanding of how different tribes' interests complement yours and how to reach agreement on working together. Your Interest Map and other preparations such as learning more about end-user expectations can help you determine how best to find out what makes members of other tribes tick. By asking questions focused on deriving crucial information, you can begin the process of establishing or improving relations with folks from different tribes within your own organization or within a larger corporate community.

Sometimes inter-tribal relations have a troubled history. In joint ventures or mergers, there's often the question of which "partner" is senior to the others. Make your preparatory assumptions. Learn all you can about the history of the relationship. Pay close attention to what members of other tribes reveal about their customs and etiquette. While this certainly does not mean you should ignore your own interests, the better you understand where others are coming from, the greater the likelihood you'll be able to develop a positive working relationship. Find commonalties among the different tribes within your organization before any external negotiations take place. Internal conflict prior to external negotiations can undercut your

> ### The Conflict-Based Conference Call
> A high-ranking manager in a major British corporation was once given a five-minute warning that he was to participate in a conference call between his company and a major client. When he joined the call, the manager was appalled to hear his company's participants in the conference call fighting among themselves— while the client simply listened to this demonstration of how the manager's company had neglected to get its act together before the conference call.

company's credibility as well as your capacity to deliver as a negotiator.

You Can't Tell a Book by Its Cover

While there are many books and articles about cross-cultural business dealings, it is extremely risky to conclude that any commonly accepted description of the taboos that drive the behavior or response of people from a particular nationality applies to everyone you meet from that culture. The relative ease of moving from one country to another, the growth of student exchange programs, and the frequency of relocation for people employed by multinational corporations mean that more and more people have been exposed to several cultures in addition to the one into which they were born. As a consequence, it is important to be extremely careful not to assume that knowing a person's nationality gives you an accurate picture of their negotiating style.

Pigeonholing

Considering the possibility that people may behave as their appearance might lead you to believe, pay close attention to any information they provide that gives you a better understanding of their individuality. On the other hand, keep in mind the many kinds of ways people may differ in their negotiation style and in other ways of dealing with people and life. For example, in many Middle Eastern countries, haggling is an art. If your negotiation style is to cut to the chase, you may be

<table>
<tr><td>CAUTION!</td><td>**Balancing Between Pigeonholing and Ignoring Information**</td></tr>
</table>

As you draw conclusions about people based on the personal characteristics they exhibit, keep their unique qualities in mind. If you are too fast to put people into pigeonholes based on external characteristics, you may filter out information that could be crucial in your negotiation strategy. Remember that information is the fundamental asset in negotiation. Typecasting a person may present an obstacle to gaining information that could bring you closer to a wise decision.

depriving your counterpart some of the joy he is looking for in the negotiation process. Both Japan and Finland, on the other hand, are generally characterized as places where the negotiation style includes a lot of silence and eyes that won't meet yours. Whether these generalities apply in the case of the people with whom you are working is something for you to find out rather than something for you to assume. In addition to corporate tribes and nationality differences, keep your mind open to possible differences based on age, gender, and other socioeconomic characteristics that may contribute to someone's negotiation style.

Negotiation Choreography

Whether a person's negotiation style comes from their cultural background, training, or personal experience, it is important to recognize elements that are likely to smooth or obstruct the process. Generally speaking, North Americans like space between their own faces and those of people with whom they are talking. Some individuals and cultures, however, are more comfortable with less distance between speakers. If you like your space and are facing someone who keeps wanting to stand closer, you run the risk of offending the other person if you keep backing away without explanation. Being clear—or transparent—about what troubles you is important:

"I hope you won't take this personally, but I am accustomed to having more space between myself and the person with

> ### Negotiating as a Social Event
> In many societies and business sectors, it is common to make negotiation a drawn-out affair. In one model, often ascribed as unique to the Arab world's *soukh* or marketplace, a buyer never accepts a merchant's first price, often walking out of a shop after first giving the merchant a sense that he is genuinely interested in buying a particular item. The process can continue for several hours, often ending in an agreement accompanied by mint tea and conversation. We need to recognize that bargaining in the marketplace, perhaps the most rudimentary form of negotiation, enhances human relationships and can lead to a joint feeling of success on the part of both the buyer and the seller.

whom I am talking. Would you be comfortable compromising with me, creating a mutually agreeable distance between us as we talk?"

When Yes Means No

In some cultures, particularly in China and Japan, it is considered bad form to say no when a person asks for a particular outcome or whether agreement has been reached. The rules of etiquette in these cultures militate against putting another person in a position of losing face if a negotiating party gives a negative response. Of course, this approach is not the sole property of people from the Far East. Even in Western society, there are many individuals who seem incapable of giving a straight answer, particularly when that answer is negative.

When your negotiating counterpart reveals that he is not prepared to give a straightforward negative response, assert your own interest in receiving a clear reply. While it is common sense to recognize the negative content in the response "Don't call us; we'll call you," you have every right to pursue greater clarity when you are offered muddy answers. When someone says something that seems to mean "Yes," ask whether that means he is in agreement with you and how that agreement will be recorded and fulfilled. Letting people know that your ego is more troubled by a non-answer than a clear answer is an intelligent exposition of your interests. Bringing your personal concerns into the process "allows" them to respond with greater clarity.

Offense as a Cultural Barrier

As the sections in Chapter 8 on giving and taking offense indicate, it is important to be clear about issues that cause you discomfort and to be sensitive to others' hot buttons. When dealing with people from other tribes within your company, with national groups, or with any group that is different for other reasons, be careful to filter out offensive behavior on their part. If you find someone's behavior unattractive, it is crucial to keep things in context. Focus on your interests, using them as a benchmark of the progress of the negotiation. Focus on what you can learn about your counterpart's interests, separating out factors that should not bar you from reaching a good result.

Language Mistakes
Whether you are dealing with someone who is not a native speaker of your language or someone who misuses or mispronounces particular words, don't focus on the mistakes unless those mistakes change the meaning of the information you are exchanging. Ask yourself how important it is that someone says "nucular" rather than "nuclear" when you both understand what the word means. Getting upset about small issues can derail you from paying attention to the important issues and lead to a failure of the negotiation process.

Overcoming Cultural Obstacles

Sometimes the cultural differences between parties appear to present obstacles to progress in negotiation. It is unrealistic to expect your counterpart to change her or his personality or cultural orientation. Similarly, when you find yourself in a different cultural situation, don't try to be something you are not. People can tell when you are putting on an act; it undercuts your credibility and your capacity to be convincing. It is good manners to learn a few words of the language of a country in which you are hoping to do business. People appreciate it when someone has made the effort to learn how to be polite in a foreign culture. This is equally true when you are working with people from a different corporate culture. If you demonstrate an effort to understand the words and phrases that have special meaning to folks from that company, it shows your motivation to increase the mutual understanding needed for reaching a wise agreement.

Problems arise when there is conflict between cultures. An American coming from a flat-structure corporate culture dealing with an extremely hierarchical French corporation may become extremely frustrated at the progress—or lack thereof—in the negotiation process. Keep focused on why you are there, asking yourself, "How does this response or set of circumstances relate to serving my interests?" Ask questions about etiquette. Try to do reality checks on the assumptions you have made about your counterpart during your preparation process. When you ask questions, listen carefully for the real meaning.

If you take the language difference between the U.S. and U.K. as an example, you can see how important it is to be careful in your communication with people from another culture. While you may be using English as the global language of business, it is critical to check the level of common understanding almost constantly. Describe scenarios or elements of the negotiation as clearly as possible; then ask your counterpart to

Two Great Nations Divided
by a Common Language

Americans working in Britain may develop a false sense of security; after all, people in the two countries all speak a language called English. Learning that there are different meanings for the same word can be important. A very cautious lawyer with whom I used to work was always careful to protect his clients in the documents he drafted. He said he wore both a "belt and suspenders." Say that to someone in the United Kingdom and you may get a puzzled look. While suspenders hold up a man's trousers in the United States, in Britain suspenders is the name for what Americans call a garter belt.

describe how she views that idea. Make it clear that you are not giving her a language test. Your purpose is to keep checking to see whether you are both on the same page.

Deriving Information to Overcome Cultural Barriers

Remember that by focusing on interests, you have a far greater chance of negotiating wisely. If you look at interests rather than at cultural dissonance, you and other parties have a far better chance of deriving benefits from your efforts at collaborative decision-making. No matter how disparate the negotiation styles of the parties, keep asking yourself, "How does this relate to my interests?" and "What am I learning about the interests of my counterpart(s)?"

Cultural factors that appear to be a challenge become less a collection of obstacles and more like elements that add spice to your interaction.

Your Interest Map will tell you what information you need and which assumptions need a reality check. Your negotiation tactics may be affected by cultural issues and the way you ask questions may be impacted by cultural characteristics, but your search for the interests of other parties will keep you from losing sight of your objectives and the interests that underlie them.

Keep in mind that cultural barriers may not relate at all to nationality. Your negotiations with people from different corporate cultures, different tribes within your own organization, or members of other generations should all be undertaken with an open mind. In addition to keeping an open mind, be careful to analyze whether the challenges you face are central to the substance of the negotiation or merely different perceptions or habits that relate to tribal or cultural differences.

How Not to Handle Cultural Dissonance

We are often tempted to try to convert people to our way of looking at things. It is easy to assume, "If it works for me/my company/my country, I'm sure it will work for them." You need to know whether trying to make "them" more like "you" is relevant to any of your interests. Negotiation is a process by which people exchange things of value in a civilized manner. Viewing negotiation as a process by which parties trade away their cultural values does not make a great deal of sense.

Getting into the heads of other parties does not mean giving them a brainwashing. Fighting another person's cultural mindset may be viewed as an attack on her self-image. This can turn off her interest in negotiating with you. People will not buy into an approach that asserts that their viewpoint or habits are inferior.

Rather than negotiating with your teenager about his taste in music, negotiate about logistical issues such as how loud the music can be played, when it can be played, and where it cannot be played. When two parties spend their energy trying to drown out each other's ideas, we get Dueling Monologues with no real negotiation taking place.

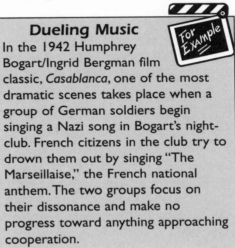

Dueling Music

In the 1942 Humphrey Bogart/Ingrid Bergman film classic, *Casablanca*, one of the most dramatic scenes takes place when a group of German soldiers begin singing a Nazi song in Bogart's nightclub. French citizens in the club try to drown them out by singing "The Marseillaise," the French national anthem. The two groups focus on their dissonance and make no progress toward anything approaching cooperation.

Can I Depend on Them?

Americans may take for granted that "a contract is a contract is a contract." In other cultures, where different laws govern contracts or different cultural norms influence the likelihood of fulfillment of a contract, you need to focus on ways to test whether another party will fulfill his or her promises. Even between American negotiation counterparts, agreements that used to be settled on a handshake now need to be backed up with elaborate legal documentation.

In all negotiations, it is necessary to build long-term fulfillment into the agreement during the process. Agreeing on incentives and penalties and deciding who determines whether the parties are keeping their side of the bargain belongs in every negotiation process. When working with people with whom you don't have an ongoing relationship or a shared history, using confidence-building measures as a mechanism for testing their commitment can be a significant means for strengthening the ultimate agreement.

Don't Get Hung Up on Style

A negotiator's central obligation is to keep focused on interests, comprehending his or her own and developing an understanding of the other parties' interests. Differences in communication styles occur between men and women, between people from cultures who want to cut to the chase and folks from cultures that weave a stylized veil over information, and between co-workers whose different tribal cultures derive from their job. Get past those differences by asking questions to derive information that will help you understand the interests of all parties and will separate cultural noise from significant issues.

In a strange environment where you are not familiar with the etiquette, you can learn by observing although it is helpful to ask for advice about expressions or customs that may throw the negotiations off course. Constantly ask yourself how a given element of the negotiation impacts on your interests and on your BATNA.

An old friend of mine used to say, "Don't get hung up on style." By using the negotiation process to develop a better understanding of your interests and the interests of the other parties and finding creative ways to get people (including yourself) to think out of the cultural box, you won't be trapped into thinking that the people with whom you are negotiating are the problem. Instead, focus on the substantive problems that you and the other negotiators hope to solve to help everyone reach a mutually agreed-upon decision.

Manager's Checklist for Chapter 9

❑ Cross-cultural negotiation occurs between people of different nationalities, between corporate cultures, and between tribes within companies. Don't expect everyone to think the same way you do.

❑ Good internal negotiations are the key to effective negotiations with outsiders. Unless your teammates are in agreement with the fundamental elements of your negotiation strategy and aspirations, they may not buy into the resulting deal with outside customers or suppliers.

❑ Listen closely to the interests and concerns of members of other tribes within your organization. Don't be afraid to ask questions.

❑ In the global market, be careful not to limit your expectations about people from other countries to stereotypes. People who have been exchange students, moved among corporate divisions, or simply traveled a lot may not be "pure" examples of what you expect based on their nationality.

❑ When cultural differences pose a potential barrier to agreement, focus on your interests to keep the process on track. If those differences seem to interfere with understanding, ask questions aimed at clarifying the issues under discussion.

❑ An open mind can help you deal with challenges posed by cultural differences.

❑ Make sure you and other negotiators comprehend and accept what makes an agreement binding.

❑ Look for potential pitfalls in the long-term fulfillment of an agreement and address them during the negotiation.

❑ Recognize that cultural differences are simply "noise"; don't confuse noise with meaningful substantive obstacles to agreement.

Creativity and Bargaining Chips

The bigger the pie, the more there is to share.
                    —old folk saying

Single-Issue Negotiating

Sometimes in a negotiation it is simplest to focus on a single issue. Very often that single issue is money. The problem with focusing on money—or on some other relatively narrow factor—is that it reduces the flexibility that parties can bring to their efforts to reach agreement. In any negotiation, it is important to expand the issues under consideration to increase the likelihood that every party will find something they can consider a gain as a result of the process.

Money is not the only thing that makes the world go 'round. Many factors can influence parties' decisions to agree with each other. More crucial than money is learning the value a party places on a given item or result. An employment compensation package has a total dollar value. Health or life insurance, a company car, an office with windows, or a job's title in addition to the salary may be of great value to one party and not so important to another.

Negotiating about a single, narrowly defined issue limits the freedom of all parties to develop solutions that respond to the variety of everyone's interests—the parties themselves, their constituents, and other stakeholders. Other stakeholders can include competitors of the negotiating parties, regulatory agencies, or neighbors of a proposed facility who are concerned about noise or the traffic it might generate. If you pursue the strategy suggested by your Interest Map, you should be able to find a variety of interests that can be served by your negotiation. Thinking about such interests as ego, reputation, or the desire of indirect stakeholders to preserve control over their own budget can help you develop a better agreement. The opportunity to use out-of-the-box thinking increases the likelihood that more interests will be met, resulting in a more durable agreement.

> **Compromise**
>
> When a negotiation hinges on a single issue or on a narrow range of issues, you may think that the simplest way to reach agreement is to compromise. There are two definitions of the "perfect" compromise. The first says that each party leaves the bargaining table equally happy. The other definition, however, should raise a red flag. It says that the result of a perfect compromise is that everyone leaves the table equally angry. And if negotiators are angry with the result, they may be reluctant to fulfill their commitments.

Multi-Issue Negotiations

Most negotiations are not limited to a single issue. Each party has his or her own interests to pursue and most likely has developed a favorite approach for getting those issues addressed. Odds are that the negotiation will cover a variety of issues rather than being limited to just one. In some cases, each issue for negotiation will be treated as a separate agenda item, with one being dealt with at a time. Other negotiations will be less structured, particularly when parties have differing priorities among their interests. The table may be covered with multiple issues all up for discussion at the same time. In a single negotiation process, you may find yourself considering product specifications, marketing, purchase of raw materials, dependability of various elements of the manufacturing and supply chain, and how to convince different tribes within your organization to agree on priorities. Whether the multi-issue negotiation is highly structured or has the appearance of chaos, keep your own interests and BATNA in mind. In addition, keep your eyes and ears on the items or assets under discussion. Elements that may be valuable to one party may not be of interest to others. If you can figure out which solutions will appeal to which party or parties, you will increase the chances of arriving at a wise agreement. Think of the items that constitute the goodies parties can exchange in the negotiation as bargaining chips.

Key Term

Bargaining chips One way to refer to the variety of items about which parties can negotiate. Bargaining chips have value to both parties—sometimes more to one of the parties than to the other—and this is what makes them useful in negotiations. Bargaining chips can include such factors as speed of delivery, who gets credit for what, and trade-offs involving specifications versus costing.

The more bargaining chips there are, the greater the likelihood that there will be something for each party to gain from the negotiation. Thus, a good negotiator uses creative thinking to bring as many bargaining chips to the process as possible. Rather than relying on standard operating procedure, going out of the box or pushing the envelope can increase the gains available to the negotiating parties. This approach can mean that each party walks away with more goodies in his or her pocket and feels more satisfied with the result.

The Value Creation Curve

In Figure 10-1, the vertical line represents the possible gains I can aim to achieve in a negotiation situation and the horizontal line represents your possible gains. If each of us pays attention only to our own interests, we may pursue a negotiation that yields a win/lose outcome. The problem with this outcome is that if a negotiation yields a winner and a loser, the person who has lost may not feel committed to fulfill his or her obligations under the agreement. Since the measure of success of a negotiation is whether it yields an agreement that the negotiating parties are committed to fulfill, obviously a win/lose result is a failure.

Value creation curve
Negotiation theoreticians often refer to this as the Pareto curve, named for the Italian economist Vilfredo Pareto. A more accurate name for the concept is value creation curve. The value creation curve describes a graphic means for plotting the most efficient possible results from negotiation. We can think of the value creation curve as illustrating the possibility of increasing the gains available to negotiators who use their creativity to expand the number of bargaining chips available to the negotiating parties.

Generally speaking, people tend to negotiate within the triangle described by the lines representing my possible gains,

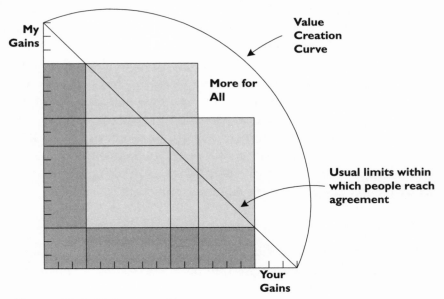

Figure 10-1. Value creation curve

Expanding the Pie

One simple way of looking at expanding the possibilities is to consider the size of an apple pie. A very small pie presents the likelihood of a zero-sum outcome. It may be enough for one person, but if two people are sharing it, neither may get enough to be satisfied. Baking—or buying—a larger pie increases the likelihood that more people will have a chance at gaining the satisfaction of enjoying a generous piece of the pie. Think of the larger pie as representing the additional possibilities found by using the concept of the value creation curve; that is, expanding the number of bargaining chips so that more parties can gain from the negotiation.

your possible gains, and the line between my maximum possible gains and your maximum possible gains. By using creativity to bring additional goodies into consideration by the negotiators, we expand the possibilities. That expansion area, which goes beyond the usual limitations of negotiators' imaginations, is the curved line that describes the value creation curve. By going out on the value creation curve, we can increase the likelihood of mutual gains and reduce the chance of a win/lose outcome.

To increase the likelihood of successful negotiation, all parties have to be prepared to reach an agreement that responds to the differing interests represented. This means that in addition to focusing on my own interests, I must accept that you will focus on getting your interests served. Unless that happens, the resulting imbalance could blow the deal between us. Using the value creation curve as a guide to our negotiation planning, we can build this understanding: In order to translate my gains or your gains into something that will really be delivered, it is a good idea to increase the likelihood that each of us will walk away feeling committed to fulfill the agreement.

Value Versus Price

Creativity in negotiation often reflects the understanding that price and value can be very different. Price is virtually always measured in money terms. Value, on the other hand, reflects how much a party desires a given result.

When you're negotiating with a counterpart, it is extremely important to find out how much she values each element about which you are bargaining. If my apple trees have produced heavily and I offer her a bag of apples saying, "Take them, I can't stand the sight of them," the offer is devalued in her eyes. On

> ### Value
> Our suburban house came with several apple trees. Some years we get a bumper crop, far more than we can eat before the apples start to rot. In a bumper crop year, I can get pretty lazy about picking hard-to-reach apples. On the other hand, when our crop is small, I value each apple so much that I'll go to extra lengths for each one I can pick from the trees.

the other hand, if I ask her whether she would like some fresh-picked homegrown apples, I'm letting her tell me how much she values them and not forcing my valuation on her.

Don't Dictate Value

If there is one consistent message throughout this book, it is that treating others with respect is necessary to make negotiation work. One of the ways you can make it clear that other parties' contributions to the development of a solution are important is to rely on them to indicate the value of something to them. This is a reasonably simple sign of respect; it is also a most pragmatic way of encouraging them to buy into the process.

We are all accustomed to advertisements telling us that Product X is the very best, that it will solve all of our problems

> ### Creating Value
> A successful preparation process will help you prioritize your interests and objectives. You may think of some issues likely to arise in the negotiation that could be agreeable for you to gain but are really not that high a priority. Later in the negotiation, you may offer to trade away your gain on those items for elements that are a higher priority for you. By negotiating seriously for less important gains, you can give your counterpart more satisfaction when you give back one gain in return for another that is more important to you.

> **△!△** **CAUTION!** **Another View of Creating Value**
> You walk a very fine line when you create value in an element of a negotiation with the expectation of trading it away for something more valuable to you. Be careful not to be manipulative. The purpose of creating value for future give-aways or concessions is to develop a negotiation element that will yield a sense of satisfaction on the part of the other negotiating parties. If what you do is perceived as manipulative—creating a phony sense of an element's value—this will damage your credibility both short- and long-term.

and keep the kids quiet, too. Most people take that kind of advertising with a grain of salt. We do not like to be told how highly we should value something; we can make our own decisions. Your Interest Maps will be built on assumptions that include what you believe about other parties' sense of the value of a given item or outcome. Remember that your assumptions are there for testing. Ask questions and observe responses using your eyes and ears to discern how highly the parties value a given possible result. As you learn how much value another party assigns to a possible result, you can figure out whether accepting that valuation will serve your interests better than trying to impose your own sense of that bargaining point's value.

Someone who tells another person, "This item is terrific. You've got to be soft in the head not to want three dozen," is being positional as well as failing to give the other person a chance to contribute his own view on the matter. If you have all the answers, there's no reason to negotiate. Your message under those circumstances to other parties is "You don't have anything to contribute to this decision." Remember that negotiation is a process for deriving benefits from working collaboratively. Don't try to force your valuations of given elements in a negotiation on other parties. While it might be of demonstrable assistance to the achievement of your interests, the forceful approach can turn off other parties and create an obstacle to reaching agreement.

When you discover that different parties view specific negotiation elements as having differing values, you have an opportunity to use your creativity to suggest solutions that reflect those differences. Think of how what you have learned can be used to expand the pie to yield results that appeal to a larger number of interested parties. Agreements that include creative solutions often have a greater value than those based on standard operating procedure.

> **Comprehending Value** Smart Managing
>
> Take particular care to understand how your negotiation partners value a given possible outcome. Listen for points they repeat as they speak, notice issues about which they raise their voices, and pay attention to the way they respond to your questions. Each of these elements of communication provides information about how significant a value they place on items on the bargaining table.

Separating People from the Problem

By definition, interest-based negotiation focuses on interests rather than on the people or parties whose interests they may be. Use your creativity to depersonalize the process and focus on the problem to be solved rather than on the parties involved. Wasting energy on "killing off" people who seem to be in the way is probably not going to gratify your fundamental interests. Consider your BATNA: "Do I really have to deal with this party?" is an important question to ask yourself. If the answer is yes, focus on your interests and the problems that need to be solved, and think of other negotiating parties as members of your problem-solving team.

Healing Relationships

People often discover that no matter what they are discussing, the process of the argument is essentially the same. A person who has a reputation for being unapproachable may be that way no matter who approaches him or what subject matter is discussed. In family relationships where subject matter may vary, arguments between spouses tend to boil down to trading accusations, whether it is about taking too long getting dressed

Creative Problem Solving

TOOLS Using a creative approach to the negotiation process can open the door to solutions that respond to the interests of many parties. The process can be made more creative in several ways:

- Brainstorm. An idea can be good no matter who suggests it. Write all the ideas on flipcharts or white boards. Only after the collective imagination is exhausted can the parties begin to throw out ideas that don't respond to interests and then refine good ideas into better ones.
- Rather than sitting on opposite sides of the bargaining table, sit on the same side. By changing from the classic situation of having the negotiating table represent a battlefield across which negotiators face each other, this approach underscores the value of collaboration, using joint efforts to pursue the interests of the negotiating parties. The symbolism of sitting side by side to act as allies can improve the process significantly.
- Experiment with out-of-the-box solutions. Don't let inhibitions keep good ideas bottled up. There is no such thing as a stupid question (although there can be stupid answers).
- Use the one-text approach. Take the thoughts of each party into account and then prepare a single document that outlines a possible resolution. Give each party a chance to comment on the document or to edit it. As President John F. Kennedy said, "Victory has a thousand fathers. Defeat is an orphan." Sharing success can be a creative procedure that brings about buy-in and commitment—and a durable agreement.

for social events or taking out the garbage. If the argument process is in a rut, even though the substantive elements of conflict may be resolved, the predictability of the process can impinge on improving business or personal relationships.

Creative approaches to changing the decision-making process can modify the way people approach an immediate problem and may help heal a challenged relationship. Whether there is difficulty in a business relationship or a personal relationship, use your imagination to recognize which interests of yours are really at stake. While it may provide short-term satisfaction to trade accusations, over the long term your desire for a productive relationship is likely to be a higher priority interest. Forcing yourself to examine where you are really coming from may not sound creative, but can require a significant investment in out-of-the-box self-examination to reach an understanding about which interests deserve higher—or lower—priorities.

Check the Appeal of Creative Elements—One by One

Your Interest Map provides you with a range of assumptions to check as you look for common ground upon which to build an agreement. In addition, a well thought-out Interest Map is the result of creative thinking: You have looked for possible interests and connections that may not be obvious if standard operating procedure is the driving force in your thought process. Finding unexpected connections or solutions requires creativity on your part and is likely to trigger creativity, or at least some degree of surprise, in the mind of your negotiation counterparts.

If your negotiation strategy contains a number of creative elements such as new ways to solve problems or overcome a climate of distrust, a cautious approach makes excellent sense. You and the other negotiators should head in two directions:

- First, commit to the big picture by agreeing that you want to agree.
- The second direction is to examine each new idea one by one to weed out potential deal breakers. It may well be that the overall concept you propose sounds good to other parties, but they may have hot buttons that lead to specific elements of the overall deal causing problems.

When you propose a creative package, be careful to offer it as an overall menu rather than a take-it-or-leave-it positional proposal. It makes no sense to lose the entire agreement because of elements that are easy for you but troublesome to other parties.

Don't Hog the Credit

Try to strike a reasonable balance between your ego and other interests of yours that drive the negotiation. In mediation, which can be viewed as negotiation stage-managed by a disinterested third party, mediators pride themselves on creating ideas for which the negotiating parties take credit. Good mediators are more interested in bringing about resolution than they are in being thought of as the problem solver. The same motivation should govern your behavior as a negotiating party.

You are negotiating with Joe Bloggs because he can contribute to satisfying some or many of your interests. Don't compete with Bloggs for credit for good ideas, particularly if you can increase his commitment to the overall agreement by allowing him to take credit. This is not to say that you should overplay the humility card. People feel more comfortable negotiating with folks who make meaningful contributions to the ultimate result. Find ways to

I Win, You Lose

Keep reminding yourself that negotiation is not a competitive sport. Focus on your own interests and the interests of your constituencies. If your ego wins credit while your counterpart's ego feels under-appreciated, chances are that the agreement will not be fulfilled and the negotiation will fail. Give credit where it is due, rather than focusing on taking credit for creative ideas.

help your counterpart devise creative responses. The creativity that you spark in him or her may well go beyond what you've already thought of and could lead to a better agreement. Share credit for a good agreement rather than hogging credit for an element. Putting too much emphasis on your ego can easily risk turning off your counterpart.

Confirming Mutual Understanding

It is particularly important to make certain that creative ideas don't muddy the waters. Throughout the negotiation process, find gentle ways of ascertaining whether the point you've made is clear. Asking questions like the following are less likely to be viewed as a test of your counterpart's comprehension than a question like "What did you just hear me say?" Instead, try these:

• How would you summarize my suggestion to your boss?

- Can you describe how this approach can be implemented?

Similarly, when other parties make proposals, check to make sure your understanding of their ideas is accurate. The question: "Am I correct in understanding that you think the project would work better in Ohio than Florida?" indicates that you have been listening and gives you an opportunity to test whether your counterpart shares your take on what you have heard.

Mutual understanding is critical. If you and other parties each think you're discussing or agreeing to different things, there is no agreement. Moreover, keeping track of understanding as the negotiation progresses is a powerful mechanism for checking whether there is real buy-in on each element of the deal. Keeping track of the negotiators' step-by-step buy-in will tell you whether the agreement will fall apart after you've shaken hands or whether it will endure for its intended lifespan.

Open Your Mind and Expand the Possibilities

Bringing more bargaining chips to the process, opening your mind to out-of-the-box thinking both in your preparation and in your response to other parties' proposals increases the likelihood of an agreement that yields more for everyone. The phrase win/win is overused, but unless parties feel they have gained from participating, there's no deal at the end of the negotiation. Listen to yourself and to others, searching all the time for seeds that can germinate into ideas that work.

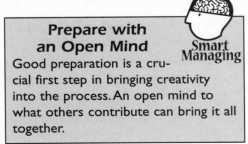

Prepare with an Open Mind

Smart Managing

Good preparation is a crucial first step in bringing creativity into the process. An open mind to what others contribute can bring it all together.

Manager's Checklist for Chapter 10

❏ Many negotiations appear to revolve around a single issue, often money or which party ends up with a particular asset. When it's money, compromise may be the least complex way to arrive at agreement. If money is simply a way of measuring the financial elements of an overall package, then compromise is a risky problem-solving approach.

❑ In negotiations where the parties are concerned with multiple issues or interests, it is the negotiators' job to look for balance among each party's priorities in order to craft a durable agreement.

❑ Whether you think of using the value creation curve or expanding the pie, each negotiator should try to add value to the process by thinking out of the box. Your Interest Map can help you spot opportunities for creating value by going beyond standard operating procedure in developing your agreement.

❑ Think of the elements considered in your negotiations as bargaining chips. The more goodies available for the parties to exchange, the greater the likelihood that each negotiator will find something to gain.

❑ Do not confuse price and value. The price is what you pay; the value is what you receive. Value is not always measured in dollars; personal satisfaction or tastes may be more significant than the amount of cash involved.

❑ When value is under discussion, don't tell other parties how valuable you think a given bargaining chip should be to them. Let them be the judge. Someone focused on cash flow will probably place a different value on fast payment than a person whose major interest is meeting a sales quota.

❑ Your negotiations are aimed at serving your interests. If you keep that focus rather than allowing another party's personality to bog down the process, you are more likely to reach a rewarding result. Don't let someone else's personality blind you to the real reason you're negotiating with them.

❑ When you add creative elements to a negotiation, whether based on your experience, your imagination, or your preparation, don't be surprised if other parties need to go through the ideas one by one. Expecting other negotiators

to accept an entire package without hesitation means you
are not negotiating with them; you are attempting to dic-
tate an outcome. They will probably resent that approach.

❏ One of the easiest things to concede is who gets the credit
for a good idea or a good deal. Unless you need to impress
your boss with your brilliance, giving or sharing credit with
your negotiation partners can be a good way to increase
their enthusiasm for the deal.

❏ Make sure you keep track of how well you and other parties understand each other. Unless you're on the same
page, your agreement may be open to conflicting interpretation down the road.

❏ If there was only one way to achieve objectives or serve
the interests that underlie them, there would be no need to
negotiate. Negotiation works because parties recognize the
value of one another's contributions. Your preferred means
for serving your interest may not be as good as an idea
coming from another party.

The Negotiation Process

Information is the fundamental asset in negotiation.

The preceding chapters have described elements and ideas that need to be considered in preparing for and utilizing negotiation to create wise agreements. This chapter explores elements of the negotiation process that can contribute to the effectiveness of the interaction among the negotiating parties. Keep in mind that every negotiation is different and that negotiations don't always follow the same script. While each of the elements of the process needs to be considered prior to and during negotiation, some may be more relevant than others in a given situation. For example, you may need to decide whether you are more concerned about getting on the same page, developing trust, or figuring out the range of possible items you can trade to make a good agreement.

Agenda Setting

You need to have a clear understanding of the agenda items that will be subject to negotiation. When negotiations sneak up on you because you bump into someone in the corridor or because you answer the phone without planning to negotiate, you will probably not have an agenda in mind. The practice of organizing agendas when you do have time to plan will enhance your skills to set an agenda on the fly and to prioritize issues.

Your preparation agenda-setting process will give you a good idea of the substantive elements a negotiation should cover in order to respond to your interests—and what you assume to be the interests of other negotiating parties and outside stakeholders. Consider the importance and priority of each item on the agenda. Look at the potential strategic consequences of the order in which issues are to be discussed.

Timing of Agenda Items

If you have decided that you want to create value in a relatively unimportant element in the negotiation in order to trade it away later for a more important objective, consider timing in proposing the negotiation agenda. If you bargain about your most important issues at the beginning and don't reach an agreement that works well in terms of your interests, it may limit the overall value of the deal even if you get everything you want in your lower priority objectives later on.

Sharing the Agenda-Building Process

Working with your counterparts in setting the agenda before the negotiation goes forward is an initial step for learning about their priorities as well as whether they wish to address issues you may not have considered. Similarly, if your counterparts make it clear that they do not want certain issues included in the agenda, you have to decide whether inclusion or exclusion responds to your interests and whether you need to negotiate about that part of the development of the agenda.

Size of the Cages

Let's say you and I are considering establishing a boarding kennel for pets whose owners cannot take them on vacation. If my focus is cats and yours is dogs, the size of the cages, runs for the animals, and other issues will have an impact on the dimensions of the facility, its design, and its cost. We need to know ahead of time whether we're both discussing the same project.

Common efforts at developing the agenda will give you and your counterparts an opportunity to practice reaching agreement. Choosing the time when particular issues should be raised is an important exercise in collaboration. As the agenda-creating process goes forward, consider how what you learn stacks up against your walking-in BATNA. Then decide whether it sounds as if you and your counterparts are likely to be able to work together. Joint agenda setting also gives you a chance to make sure that you and your counterparts are on the same page. Why waste your time negotiating with parties who have such a different view of what's important that you'll always be talking at cross-purposes?

You Can't Tell the Players Without a Scorecard

Your efforts with other negotiators to develop an agenda prior to the sit-down negotiation should yield a written document that all relevant participants bring to the negotiation. It may well be that only the lead negotiators have copies. On the other hand, if several people are involved and each participant has the written agenda, each person can see when his or her substantive focus is likely to become the issue under discussion.

A written agenda in hand increases the likelihood that participants in the negotiation process will get a sense of the big picture. It can be frustrating to deal with a participant whose focus is so narrow that he is an obstacle to the forward momentum of the negotiation. Understanding where everyone's issue fits within the overall situation helps keep things in context, with proper priority given to issues as they arise during the discussion.

The Agenda: First Draft of the Agreement

The written agenda can serve as a guide to the progress of the negotiation. An intelligent step is to summarize agreements reached on each agenda item—even if the details of those agreements will require spelling out at a later time. Sophisticated negotiators ask the participants to initial next to the summaries of agreements reached on each agenda item. While this does not create a legally binding contract, it does create a record of the progress.

If you create an agenda with summarizations, give photocopies of the document to the participants at the end of the session. When everyone has a copy of the same information, no one can accuse others of changing any elements. If I want to be sneaky and change the original document, my attempts to make changes will lose all credibility if you have a copy of the original.

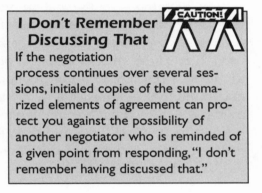

I Don't Remember Discussing That

If the negotiation process continues over several sessions, initialed copies of the summarized elements of agreement can protect you against the possibility of another negotiator who is reminded of a given point from responding, "I don't remember having discussed that."

Using the Agenda as a Process for Benchmarking

One of the crucial issues in negotiation is whether the parties can count on the resulting agreement to be durable. Remember that the test of a negotiation's success is whether the parties reach an agreement that each party is committed to fulfill. In the process of agreeing on an agenda, you and your negotiating partners have an opportunity to create benchmarks to determine whether everyone is acting in good faith in terms of the process itself, during the creation of the agenda as well as in the "official" negotiation. If you and other parties cannot agree on the order in which items will be discussed, that can give you a sense of how hard it may be to reach an agreement with them.

> **Unexpected Agenda Changes**
>
> **Smart Managing** If the parties to a negotiation have agreed in advance on an agenda, you need to monitor whether anyone tries to delete an agreed-upon item from the discussion or add something new that you have agreed not to discuss (or something you had not contemplated at all). If you agree to the deletion or addition, however, the negotiation remains a mutually agreed upon process. On the other hand, if you disagree with the addition or deletion and another party insists that it should be part of the negotiation, you need to consider whether this is a sign of bad faith that reduces your confidence in the long-term credibility of that party.

Use both the agenda-creating process and the negotiation itself as a means for measuring whether you can count on other parties to keep their word. The agenda-creation process can be used to build the habit of reaching agreement with one another, to measure the likely long-term dependability of various parties, and to develop or improve a relationship. Working together on a mutually agreed upon agenda can make the negotiation process move more smoothly and efficiently. Sharing the effort of agreeing on an agenda before negotiation can also be used as a confidence-building measure.

Building Confidence and Comfort

Building confidence among negotiating parties is often an important first step—or series of steps—that needs to be undertaken before the substantive negotiation can begin. It may be as simple as starting off the process with a cup of coffee or having a meal together. Use these activities as opportunities to get acquainted with someone you don't know or with whom you initially feel uncomfortable.

Confidence-building measures can be more elaborate. The parties can negotiate in phases, trading agreements and performance on a piece-by-piece basis. As each small agreement is fulfilled, the parties can work on larger, more complex or more divisive issues. Early demonstrations that agreements made become agreements fulfilled can increase all parties' confidence that the overall process will be worthwhile. In each of these stages of the negotiation you should examine your BATNA to see how it is changed by what you learn about other parties or by their fulfillment or failed fulfillment of promises. Figure out ways to examine the behavior of the other parties to gain a

Building confidence
When negotiating parties do not know each other well or if they have an unfriendly history, they can use a variety of tools to increase their comfort level with one another. In international diplomacy, these are often referred to as confidence-building measures. Asking good questions and listening carefully are confidence-building elements in any negotiation.

sense of what you can expect from them over the long term.

Utilizing Your Interest Map

Your preparation before negotiation includes both the homework you do to become more familiar with the subject matter and your development of an Interest Map that reflects your assumptions about the interests of the negotiating parties, their constituencies, and other stakeholders. Use your Interest Map as a guide throughout the negotiation process; it should tell you what kinds of information you need to get from others in order to reach a wise agreement.

Your Interest Map does not provide you with a strategy or tactics that are set in stone. Remember that it is based on assumptions and homework—your assumptions may not be 100 percent accurate.

The Purpose of Communication
Remember that people would rather be listened to than lectured at. Using the Interest Map as an outline of questions rather than as the skeleton of the perfect solution, will help you become a better audience and thus learn more from your counterparts. The more information you can glean from them, the greater your ability to assess how your BATNA is affected by what you learn and the greater your ability to respond creatively and effectively to the information you gain from their answers to your questions.

> ### Interest Map Strategies and Tactics
>
> While it is up to you to decide whether to include the physical Interest Map among your papers during the negotiation process, keep the questions it raises in mind as your negotiation goes forward, whether you have it with you or not.
> - Do a reality check on the assumptions you have made about the various stakeholders.
> - Use your Interest Map questions to develop a better sense of what kind of priority each negotiator places on his or her various interests.
> - Figure out whether the connections among interests you assumed during the creation of your Interest Map will, in fact, lead to an agreement that responds to the interests and priorities of stakeholders.
> - Remember, if one or more of your pre-negotiation assumptions fails the reality test, it does not mean everything you have considered is wrong.
> - When another party comes up with what appears to be a surprise—or what she thinks may surprise you—check whether your Interest Map has prepared you for that specific possibility or whether it can give you hints on how to respond.

Look at your preparation as a means for increasing your understanding of your own situation and as an outline of what you need to learn from other negotiating parties in order to develop a mutual agreement that the various parties are willing to fulfill. The Interest Map is more an outline of questions to ask than a definer of answers.

Bargaining

People use many words to describe various approaches to negotiating: bargaining, dickering, trading, and haggling are a few. While the different terms bring different styles to mind, the underlying fact is that, as a result of a fair negotiation process, parties derive benefits from the input or contributions of other parties.

Is Everything Open to Bargaining?

There are some people who just have to get the best deal, no matter what the situation. Television commercials play on that desire. If you buy this car, you'll get a better warranty, price, features, and so on than if you buy a car from the competition. Among the questions we have to ask ourselves is whether we are comfortable haggling over everything and whether we are comfortable with people who are never satisfied. Do you want to be known in business or in your personal

> **Negotiation** A process by which people exchange goods or other things of value in a civilized manner. Negotiation offers us the opportunity to "wage peace" to reach the right agreement. Interest-based negotiation is not a zero-sum game yielding a winner and a loser, but rather a process by which parties contribute to the creation of an agreement that makes sense to them.

life as someone who always tries to gain the advantage over others?

Your reputation, both personal and professional, must be taken into account when you decide how hard to push and whether you have to negotiate over everything. You need to determine when negotiation is likely to yield a better result. If you are shopping at a garage sale or in some other place where haggling is expected by buyers and sellers, it is foolish not to attempt to walk away with a better deal. In business, pay close attention to the tolerance level of your negotiation counterparts. They may shy away from dealing with you in the future if you keep pushing for more, just as being overly positional can be a turn-off in a negotiation. Understanding your BATNA gives you a sense of the value of turning a transaction into a bargaining session. Sometimes you discover good reasons to look for something in return for your inconvenience.

If ... Then ...

We must consider the form our bargaining will take. When we present a take-it-or-leave-it position, the only way we can back away from that positional approach is to lose face. Presenting an offer with an incentive is far more likely to bring negotiators to an agreement with which each party feels comfortable. After listening carefully to the information presented by our counter-

Free Drinks for Long Waits

Two examples from my own life illustrate the choices available to parties on different sides of the bargaining table:

1. Many years ago my family had a confirmed reservation at a restaurant on a resort island for dinner at 7:30 P.M. We arrived on time, but were told that the restaurant had not set aside a table and that we would have to wait. There were 15 of us, ranging in age from two years old to a couple in their 80s. We were upset at the inconvenience caused by the restaurant's poor planning. I politely told the headwaiter that, particularly given the age range of our party, we were troubled at having to wait. My suggestion was that everyone in our family should be given a drink on the house to compensate for our inconvenience. After some thought, the headwaiter agreed and we were accommodated while waiting for the table to be readied.

2. More recently, my wife and I had dinner (without reservations) at a Japanese restaurant in our town. We patiently waited for a table. Once seated, the food came very slowly; obviously the kitchen was overburdened. Our waitress did not wait for us to ask; she brought us an extra carafe of hot *sake* on the house.

In the first example, we were obviously inconvenienced by the restaurant's poor planning. In the second, you could argue that no one was at fault. But the voluntary compensation in the Japanese restaurant will build our loyalty as customers far more than the effort we had to expend negotiating for free drinks at the resort's restaurant.

parts and developing a better informed sense of their interests and priorities, we are better able to make offers that should be appealing to them.

One method of offering a bargain or trade that often works to bring people to agreement is to suggest the give-and-take elements that are in play: "If you promise to give me a book I need to read to increase my skills, then I will reward you with a letter of reference that can go into your personnel file and help advance your career."

Presenting an offer as an If ... Then ... proposal gives your counterpart a chance to see how her reward is linked to your achievement of your objective. Making the trading process transparent can increase the parties' confidence in the value of the deal as well as the dependability of each other. Clearly, should I arrive with the letter of reference in hand at the appointed time and you arrive without the promised book, I can withhold delivery of the letter until you have fulfilled your part of the bargain.

Characterizing elements of the negotiation process as trade-offs can make the purpose of the activity clearer. When you use the If . . . Then . . . approach, there is clear communication between the parties; everyone is on the same page, at least for that element of the negotiation.

Building Long-Term Commitment

Except in rare instances—for example, when you are bargaining for a souvenir with a street vendor—creating an agreement that will endure over a specific length of time is a crucial part of negotiation. In your preparation, think about whatever might go wrong, short- or long-term, and keep those concerns in mind when you negotiate.

In addition to taking the preventive medicine approach while you are negotiating in order to create a durable agreement, you

---

What Can Go Wrong

There are many kinds of glitches that can cause problems in the fulfillment of an agreement. The following list is aimed at giving you an idea of ranges of problems. Look for specific things to worry about that pertain to your situation:

- Your counterpart doesn't have the authority to bind his or her company.
- There may be a strike, a fire in a factory, or other interruptions in the capacity of a party to deliver.
- The product does not meet specifications.
- Needs or resources change during the life of the contract.
- The buyer's own customers may go out of business.
- A negotiating party is hit by a lawsuit that reduces its capacity to get financing to deliver the product contemplated in the agreement.
- Lawyers or other professionals representing one or more parties become an obstacle to agreement—even though the parties have reached agreement.

Penalties or Incentives?

Occasionally you find that agreements contain penalties for nonperformance or the failure to meet deadlines. Penalties present the risk that as they increase, the penalized party may find it less costly to pay the penalty than to fulfill the agreement. As an alternative, many agreements contain incentives for timely performance. It may be wise to have the negotiation include decisions on how much a party will be paid for delivering the goods faster or better than the minimum standards agreed upon by the negotiators.

need to consider what mechanisms you and your negotiating partners should have in place during the term of the agreement. One question to ask yourself is, "How can I be sure my counterpart is fulfilling his part of the bargain? Are there things he needs to do to monitor my performance?" It sometimes makes a lot of sense to look for a disinterested third party to monitor the performance of the parties. An objective outsider may be more credible to the parties when it comes to determining whether performance measures up to their promises.

Objective Criteria

There is a parallel element to the use of objective outsiders to monitor the quality of performance of a party to an agreement. Often negotiators run up against a "your word against mine" mentality. When negotiating parties disagree over such issues as quality, quantity, price, or similar issues, it can be quite difficult to find a way for one party to convince others that his assertion on a given issue is more accurate. In these circumstances, an outside source of information is helpful.

Finding objective criteria may be as simple as referring to a well-known publication, an encyclopedia, or a Web site. In some businesses, trade associations establish standards to help negotiators reach a conclusion. There are also professionals who are trained and certified as experts regarding such assets as jewelry, real estate, and other holdings where your word is no more convincing than my word.

The Blue Book

When a buyer and a seller are engaged in determining the fair price for a used car, they can refer to the Kelley Blue Book or similar competing publications or Web sites for unbiased information on used car pricing. Thus, when I try to sell you my 1988 Volvo with 200,000 miles on the odometer, we might disagree on the right price. If we agree to use the Kelley Blue Book as an objective source of information, we can look up the price range the book says is appropriate for a Volvo with my car's age, mileage, and accessories.

ZOPA

In the absence of a source of objective information, particularly when the parties are negotiating over price, a good idea is to look for the ZOPA—the Zone of Possible Agreement. This brings us back to the myth that the first person who mentions a financial figure loses. As you recall, the most effective way to overcome that potential obstacle to agreement is to be prepared to propose a price range within which you think the deal should be made. While it may happen that the range you suggest works for your counterparts, it is also possible that other parties' preferred price ranges will diverge from the range you propose.

> **ZOPA (Zone of Possible Agreement)** A range of prices within which the negotiating parties find they are likely to reach agreement.

You need to listen to the response to your price range proposal and determine whether it shows a ZOPA. If you and your counterpart are a million miles apart, take another look at your BATNA to figure out whether the current negotiation is worth continuing. If your BATNA tells you to continue the current negotiation, it may take creativity to find ways to add or subtract value from what you or your counterparts are offering one another in order to create a ZOPA that will lead to agreement. Focusing only on take-home pay in a salary negotiation can impede decision making. By outlining other elements of the compensation package such as health insurance, parking space, or vacation time, the parties can look for elements that create a Zone of Possible Agreement.

Expectations and Concessions

Your attention to your interests and their priority in your preparation process should help you develop a set of expectations regarding the likely outcome of the negotiation. The expectations will shape your description of specific objectives. Use language indicating that you want to achieve more without scaring off other parties. Don't express your objectives in a positional manner; it leaves you less room to bargain and creates the risk that ratcheting down those objectives means you lose face.

When you develop your expectations, plan ahead for what you are willing to concede or trade away in order to serve your interests. Concessions that are planned ahead of time are far less painful than concessions you yield under pressure. If your agreement is the result of your concession to pressure, or if your counterpart only agrees as a result of concession to your pressure, the agreement will lack the fundamental mutuality necessary to say a negotiation was successful. Unwanted concessions lead to unenforceable agreements.

Key Term

Expectation What you anticipate gaining by undertaking negotiation. Your expectations should be aggressive, but realistic and not positional. When you are negotiating a sale of your company's products, your expectations may include what you hope to achieve regarding price, quantity, specifications, and delivery.

Concession Something you have indicated you want but which you agree to forego or give up in order to reach agreement. Concessions should not be against your fundamental interest. In understanding that negotiation is a give-and-take process, you need to consider what you are prepared to give in order to achieve particular gains. Thus, if speedy delivery is your most critical interest, you may need to concede on price and pay a little extra.

Compromise

Sometimes people think that compromise is a necessary element of a negotiated agreement. When the negotiation is about a single type of bargaining chip or very small range of

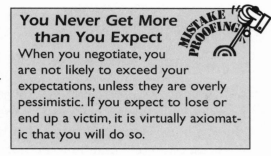

You Never Get More than You Expect
When you negotiate, you are not likely to exceed your expectations, unless they are overly pessimistic. If you expect to lose or end up a victim, it is virtually axiomatic that you will do so.

issues, compromise may yield a mutually acceptable result. On the other hand, when the negotiation is complex, with multiple assets, interests, or parties, compromise may be extraordinarily difficult. Before compromising, examine your BATNA and determine whether reaching agreement is more important than interests that must be given away in order to reach a compromise. Let's say you are offering to sell a used bicycle for $20 and I would like to buy it for $10. Price is the only issue dividing us from making the deal. If each of us agrees to compromise on a price of $15—effectively splitting the difference—we are likely to have a deal.

Compromise may be the best answer when reaching agreement is a goal that stands by itself. However, when each party is pursuing his or her interest, reaching agreement may be less valuable than protecting what you already have. Compromise is a means to an end, but should not be viewed as an end in itself.

Collaboration

The interest-based approach to negotiation works when parties looking to serve their own particular interests—and perhaps those of their constituents—find other parties who can offer the bargaining chips necessary for achieving those interests. Giving the negotiating parties the opportunity to provide assets, information, or creative ideas to assist other parties in getting their interests served requires a spirit of cooperation or collaboration. When negotiators treat one another as partners who share a desire to solve a reasonably clear range of problems using an open, fair process, their collaboration can often yield a synergetic result where the whole is greater than the sum of its parts.

Multitasking

Negotiators are people, not computers. It is accepted that computers can multitask; they easily perform more than one function at a time. People are more likely to focus on a narrow set of issues, often one at a time. In order to negotiate efficiently and effectively, you need to keep many things in your mind at once. Your preparation should open your mind to a wide variety of issues that may arise during negotiation. Understanding how each decision may have an impact on others gives you a greater likelihood of negotiating wisely. If you focus too heavily on maintaining your relationship with your negotiating partner, you may decrease the likelihood of serving your interests. Allowing another party's bullheadedness to drive you crazy may deflect you from keeping your eye on your BATNA, and you may lose an opportunity to make a better deal somewhere else. Comprehending the priority of a given agenda item will help you keep it in context so that you don't waste time or energy on less important matters.

It is easy to tell yourself to multitask, to think several moves ahead. Nonetheless, you can risk overload that can interfere with a good negotiation process. Take time out from a negotiation, particularly one that seems to be moving too fast.

Playing the Game
The most successful negotiators are like top chess or billiards players. They are not concentrating on the immediate move but rather on how the results of that move will influence the next series of moves in the game—or in the negotiation process.

Remember, fast answers can lead to long consequences. Using the time-out approach can help you gather your wits, analyze the situation, and determine whether your overall strategy or specific tactics are contributing to a wise negotiation process.

It's Not Over Until It's Over

You and the parties with whom you negotiate need to find some mutually understood way of signifying when there is closure. Whether it is a handshake, a press release, or an elaborate contract, be certain there is clear understanding that the negotiation phase of a transaction is complete.

Under contract law, an agreement can be changed if its parties agree to the changes. Contract law does not allow unilateral changes to be binding on all the parties to an agreement. Therefore, if circumstances change, it is perfectly appropriate to contact your negotiating partners and suggest that changes may be in order after the agreement or contract has been adopted. If they agree, changes are possible. If they do not agree, be sure to look at the legal and business consequences that can result if the agreed-upon contract is broken.

Using Time-Out

There are a number of ways to bring time-outs into the negotiation process to give yourself a chance to regroup and analyze the situation:

- Arrange to have time-outs scheduled at specific times during the process—coffee breaks, opportunities to check your voicemail, meetings with your teammates.
- If the negotiation is taking place in your office, perhaps conspire with a colleague to call you after, say, 45 minutes. Ask your counterpart if he would mind giving you some privacy while you take a call you've been anticipating for several days.
- Sometimes you find yourself fighting an agreement that seems to keep gathering momentum. Things move fast and you find yourself really needing a time-out. You can ask for a time-out—and perhaps your counterpart will agree. But she may say, "We've nearly reached agreement; we shouldn't quit while we're (I'm) ahead." At that point, your best choice may be to say, "I really didn't intend to say this, but actually I need to use the bathroom." No one but you can tell whether that is true; taking private time where you won't be bothered can make a real difference.

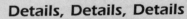

TRICKS OF THE TRADE

Details, Details, Details

If you or a counterpart think something is a small detail, don't gloss over it and say, "We'll cross that bridge if we come to it." The details you ignore during the negotiation process can have a nasty habit of sneaking up and biting you when and where you least expect it during the lifetime of the agreement.

Not Rocket Science

Negotiation is not rocket science. Everyone, even children too young to read this book, has a negotiation style. Remember that in negotiation there are always choices to make. There is no consistently right formula. Negotiation may have many stages, although the order is sometimes scrambled. Memorizing a play-book will not make you a good negotiator. Thinking about the negotiation ahead of time, focusing on your interests, and listening to other parties to understand them better will help you make more effective use of your negotiating time and increase your effectiveness and efficiency.

Manager's Checklist for Chapter 11

❑ In preparing for negotiation, figure out how you want the process to help you satisfy the objectives or interests you are pursuing.

❑ Deciding what items should be on the agenda and when they should be discussed can have a significant impact on a negotiation's outcome.

❑ Sharing the agenda-setting process with your counterpart can give you a chance to become accustomed to agreeing with each other. It can also get you onto the same page.

❑ The agreed-upon agenda can be thought of as the skeleton of the agreement toward which the parties are aiming. The agenda and any notes you make on it during the process may not be a legal document, but it can help keep the parties honest. This can provide the underpinning for monitoring the long-term fulfillment of the promises made by each party.

❏ When you're negotiating with a new party, or if parties to a negotiation have a troubled history with each other, confidence-building measures can increase the likelihood they will be able to work together.

❏ Your Interest Map is an important strategic tool. Use it to figure out what information you need in order to make a wise decision in terms of your interests and BATNA. Utilize the questions raised by your Interest Map to learn about other parties and to check off assumptions that work.

❏ You can negotiate about virtually anything, but if you treat getting a better bargain as a game you may dissuade people from wanting to deal with you. Can your interests be served better if you go with the flow?

❏ Linking items by using the If ... Then ... approach may provide your counterparts incentives to reach agreement with you.

❏ Use worst-case analysis to develop ways of measuring the performance of other parties both during negotiation and in the fulfillment of the agreement. Prepare for "what's the worst that can happen?" This will help you develop ways to conclude whether you can depend on the long-term fulfillment of your agreement with the negotiating parties.

❏ A disinterested third party or an independent source of expertise can provide objective criteria for monitoring the fulfillment of the agreement.

❏ Finding the ZOPA, the Zone of Possible Agreement, can help negotiating parties focus on a realistic bargaining range.

❏ You will do better in the give-and-take of negotiation if your expectations are aimed high enough to give you room for concessions.

❏ The object of interest-based negotiation is to collaborate to serve the parties' interests rather than to compromise just to make a deal.

❏ Try not to fall into the trap of thinking that negotiation is about one issue at a time; the interrelationship among issues and strategies needs to be considered throughout the negotiation process. If multitasking is difficult, take time-outs to give yourself a chance to analyze what's going on and what you would like to change.

The Seven Pillars of Negotiational Wisdom

Don't let the forest obscure the trees.

Paying Attention to Priorities

While negotiation should be reasonably easy, particularly if you are well prepared on the subject matter, it still requires that you pay attention to the process. Many elements of the process can influence how the negotiation goes; the challenge is choosing how to prioritize and utilize the process elements of each negotiation to fit its peculiar circumstances. The Seven Pillars of Negotiational Wisdom* lists the process elements that merit your consideration each time you negotiate. It is very important to prioritize among them, choosing which Pillars represent a higher or lower priority in each negotiation in which you participate.

The Seven Pillars

As presented in the accompanying illustration, seven elements of the negotiation process need to be considered both before a negotiation (as you prepare) and during negotiations (when you multitask or take a time-out to analyze the situation). The Seven Pillars are not in any particular order of priority; each may be the most important—or least important—process element in a given situation:

- Relationship
- Interests
- BATNA
- Creativity
- Fairness
- Commitment
- Communication

Relationship

In many of your negotiations, you may be negotiating with repeaters, whether they be business colleagues, clients or suppliers, or people with whom you deal in your personal life. The wisest approach to take, particularly when dealing with the same people time after time, is to treat each negotiation as an episode in an ongoing relationship. This view will give you the freedom to look at gains or losses from a long-term perspective.

Huh?

Walter Brady had frequent contact with a person in a very senior position in a client company. The client was embarrassed about his progressive loss of hearing, but kept "'forgetting" to wear his hearing aid. Brady dreaded their negotiations as the client would cup his hand to his ear and respond to whatever Brady was saying with "Huh?" Brady's irritation was growing, until he realized that he had to put his irritation aside. The relationship was far more important than the annoyance factor. He needed his client and his client wasn't trying to be a problem. When the priority of the relationship was established in his mind, Brady modified his negotiation planning to respond with greater consideration for his client's hearing loss.

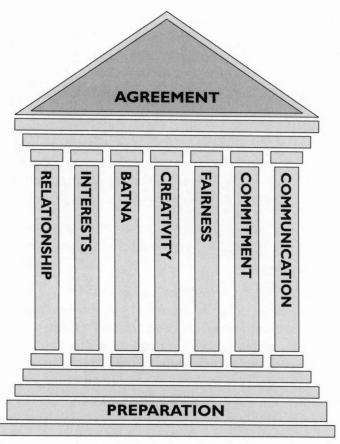

Figure 12-1. The Seven Pillars of Negotiational Wisdom

Understanding the value of the ongoing relationship can have a significant impact on how you pursue the negotiation process.

Business to Business

The importance of business relationships goes well beyond the satisfaction you derive from turning clients into friends. Developing durable positive relationships can have a direct impact on the bottom line. Maintaining good business relationships also builds your company's reputation, increases the likelihood of repeat business, and may enhance the likelihood you

The Printer's Devil

Smart Managing A printing company with which my company does a lot of business was invaded by a "devil" when it did a job for us. It produced 5,000 copies of a document with a small but annoying typographical error. When we called the problem to their attention, they offered to reprint the entire order at their expense, thus protecting the relationship. Our response was "We can live with that typo. We don't want the mistake to cost you that much money. We'll use up the 5,000 copies and depend on you to correct the typo in future printings of the document." The printer was delighted. As a result of our attitude, we always get fast service, often leapfrogging the line of other customers waiting for their printing jobs.

will get more attractive treatment in terms of price and delivery than companies without a well-established relationship.

Sales and Purchasing

People in sales need thick skins, particularly if they have to make a lot of cold calls. On the other side of the coin, purchasing agents or managers need to be relatively hard-nosed in their focus on their company's or department's interests regarding price, specifications, and delivery. Whether you are involved in sales or purchasing, develop relationships upon which you can depend. Knowing which buyers will welcome you with open arms—buyers who won't groan when you make your calls—can increase your satisfaction with your professional life.

Personal and Close Colleagues

In personal negotiations, relationship may be the overwhelming priority, especially as you interact with your spouse, your children, and your parents. Think about the importance of relationship when you feel annoyed by the habits of people with whom you are likely to be involved for most of your life. Sometimes they need to change their habits to avoid making gaffes in public. Consider carefully how to address such issues effectively without jeopardizing the relationship. Separating the person from the problem can be a critical element; it's not the person in the next office who annoys you, but rather his habit of using inappropriate language in social settings. As you may work together for a long time, consider the relationship when you address your colleague's annoying habit.

Internal Negotiation

Selling your ideas to members of different tribes within your organization can often be harder than convincing people from the outside to agree with you. Knowing who to talk to when you need to solve a problem internally and developing an efficient way of collaborating with people whose focus is different from yours will increase the likelihood that the package you offer to outsiders will work. Your relationships with colleagues will influence your internal credibility and contribute to your comprehension of what you can deliver. Paying appropriate attention to the relationships you develop and maintain with your colleagues and internal clients can pay dividends on immediate problems and increase the efficiency of the organization. While a clerk in the Accounts Payable may not seem terribly interesting to you, it

---

Bring Creativity into the Process

Smart Managing

If you think out of the box by looking at the process rather than at the substance of the argument, you may contribute to both an immediate solution to the problem and a long-term strengthening of the relationship. Take time out to ask yourself how what's going on in the negotiation should be analyzed in terms of the negotiation process rather than whether you like another party's proposal.

Negotiating with the Boss

Mistake Proofing

Sometimes your boss assigns you a task that you feel runs counter to the company's long-term interests. Don't barge in and say, "Hey, boss, that's the dumbest idea I've ever heard." Ask questions: "If the market for our product begins to weaken, how will this idea contribute to our capacity to ride out the problems?" or "How would you sell this idea to (a) possible customers, (b) the shareholders, or (c) someone from a regulatory body?" Strengthening your relationship with the boss by establishing your credibility can serve not only your personal long-term interests but also the well being of your company.

can yield real benefits to remember his name and maintain a cordial relationship with him. When one of your important suppliers is facing a cash crunch, you can use your relationship with the Accounts Payable clerk to speed up payment and increase the likelihood that your supplier will treat your company better in the future. People remember how they've been treated.

Interests

Negotiation is not a competitive sport. Each party undertakes negotiations in order to bring about the most favorable possible solution for their own interests. Getting your interests served need not mean denying others an agreement that responds to their interests. Focus on the other parties' interests as well as on your own in order to develop a better result than you could achieve without their contribution to the negotiations. The choice you have is whether to make the focus on interests a high or low priority among the elements of the negotiation process.

If interests are your high priority, you need to have a good understanding of your own interests so that you don't make fast decisions or commitments that undercut them. At the same time, comprehend as much as you can of other parties' interests in order to increase your capacity to influence the other parties by showing them how their interests have been considered as you've developed your proposals. Focusing on interests can help you overcome cultural and other obstacles to agreement. If you keep interests at the forefront of your mind, you can not only avoid regrettable decisions, you can also see beyond small and large annoyances that might block a favorable result. Keep your eyes on the prize—your interests—and the prize is far less likely to elude you.

Questions to Ask Yourself

When you first ask yourself, "What is my interest in this objective?" you are more than likely to think about why the objective is important. Take that inquiry a step further and try to figure out "Why is this objective important to me?" Since virtually

---

Finding Your Interests

When you are trying to figure out what interests lie behind the objectives you have set out for yourself, be prepared to ask yourself some serious questions. Here are a few examples:

- If my objective is not achieved, will I suffer any damage? If so, what is the damage?
- How does reaching—or failing to reach—this objective reflect on my ego? my career aspirations? my hopes for my family? the good of my company?
- What routes are available to achieve my underlying goals? If an approach that differs from my announced objective is utilized, does that threaten my interests?
- Is my interest as easy to explain to myself or to others as the goal I have chosen?
- How many alternatives are acceptable to me and why?

---

everyone considers himself to be a well-motivated person, be careful not to fall into the trap of thinking, "If this is the result I am seeking, it must be a good one."

Understanding Others' Interests

Asking good questions and doing reality checks on your assumptions should help you arrive at a better understanding of your negotiating partners' interests. The more you learn about the interests of your negotiation counterparts, the greater the likelihood you will be able to draw realistic conclusions about hidden agendas that lie behind their negotiation strategies and their objectives. Focusing on interests can also help you prioritize cultural and other potential obstacles to reaching a wise agreement. Internal tribes within companies, such as purchasing and accounting, can be viewed as representing different cultures. Purchasing people may be facing an end-user's deadline that gives them cause to pay a little extra; accounting staff are interested in controlling money. While both tribes share an interest in the bottom line, the differing mindsets or cultures will influence how they view a particular deal with an external supplier. Comprehension of your negotiating partners' interests

Other Stakeholders' Interests

The constituencies to whom you and your negotiation partners have to pay attention have interests that may have a strong influence on the interests of the negotiators. While you may have an interest in improving your reputation with your boss by delivering a good deal in terms of the bottom line, your boss may have a very separate interest, such as demonstrating her capacity to manage subordinates to the Human Resources department.

should be a critical tool in developing proposals that increase the likelihood of an agreement that brings the parties together. When your negotiation partners see that your proposals reflect what is important to them, they are far more likely to respond positively to what you suggest.

BATNA

Your preparatory work that informs you of the relative strength of your BATNA can be an extraordinarily high-priority negotiation process element. If you understand your BATNA, you have a good idea whether negotiation offers a good way to resolve the issues you face, what kind of choices you can make in terms of potential negotiation partners, and what possible information can trigger your choice to walk away from an unpromising negotiation. During your preparation, investigate which resources you control or influence that can serve your interests. This establishes the baseline of your walking-in BATNA. By figuring out what information you need in order to make wise decisions on substantive elements of the negotiation, you estab-

Not Your Bottom Line

CAUTION!

Remember that your BATNA is not your bottom line. Even in a price-focused negotiation where your bottom line dictates how far you can go in decision making, your BATNA tells you whether you have a better way to serve your interests, such as doing business with a different supplier or customer, modifying the payment process, or agreeing on financial incentives or penalties. While these sorts of choices can have an impact on the bottom line, they are also alternatives that do not lock you into a strictly price-focused approach.

lish benchmarks against which you can measure whether the process is strengthening, weakening, or changing your BATNA.

Dynamic BATNA

Because your BATNA changes during the negotiation process as you derive information from other negotiating parties, it may become more or less important as a negotiation process element. Pay attention to the way your BATNA changes depending on the information that passes back and forth during the negotiation. While you should always focus on your interests and not take any steps or make agreements contrary to your interests, your attention to changes in your BATNA offers you a tool for effective decision making. Learning that another party's ego needs a lot of attention can change your BATNA; it can give you an opportunity to make her an offer that serves your interest at very low cost to your own.

> ### Deadlines
>
> Smart Managing
>
> The deadlines that you and your negotiation counterparts face can be an important component of your respective BATNAs. Keep an eye on the clock or calendar to determine whether any of the parties' deadlines are strengthening or weakening their BATNA. If another negotiator keeps glancing at his watch, he may be revealing that he faces a pressing deadline. If this is new information to you, it could modify your understanding of the relative strengths of his BATNA and yours.

Creativity

During preparation as well as during the negotiation process, ask yourself how a creative approach could serve the interests of all the parties. When you are dealing with a positional negotiator who can't see alternatives to his or her initial proposal, creativity may become the top priority in your negotiation process. Asking good questions of an apparently impenetrable negotiator can often help you learn enough about her interests to develop proposals she is likely to find interesting and perhaps even attractive. Try to get her to respond when you ask, "What do you find about my company that makes you want to do

Thinking out of the Box

To get your creative juices running, try to remove yourself from the situation. Think about the situation you face from a different perspective—like a five-year-old, or someone who doesn't understand the language, or a stakeholder who's not at the negotiating table. When standard operating procedure is taken out of the picture, you are better able to think out of the box and bring greater creativity to the negotiation process.

business with us?" or "Are there things I should know about why you are not interested in this deal?" Questions like "What elements of my proposal are most appealing (or unappealing) to you?" or "Can you describe how you have dealt with these sorts of issues in the past?" can also open doors for your analysis of creative ways to add value that will heighten her interest in dealing with you.

More for All: The Value Creation Curve

Design your creativity to expand the possibilities available to the negotiating parties. By going out on the value creation curve, there is a greater likelihood that parties will feel as if they have gained by negotiating with one another. Remembering the value creation curve (as described in Chapter 10) is an effective way of reminding yourself to negotiate for success—to reach an agreement the parties will willingly fulfill.

Add More Bargaining Chips

Smart Managing   By increasing the number of bargaining chips under discussion, you increase the opportunities for more negotiators to gain from the process. Listen carefully to what others indicate turns them on. Find ways to introduce bargaining chips not previously under discussion to increase the likelihood that the parties will derive more potential gains from the process. While a particular kind of transaction may be resolved based on price and specifications, you may want to propose modifications in the payment process: drop shipment rather than warehouse-to-warehouse; exchange of letters of appreciation that can be filed in one another's personnel files; a ribbon-cutting ceremony involving the CEOs as value-adding bargaining chips.

Fairness

Unless the parties consider the negotiation process fair, there is
a strong risk that some negotiators will end up feeling less committed to the agreement than others. One of the problems we
face in the global marketplace is that there is no absolute universal standard for fairness. In western culture, we can view the
Golden Rule as describing fair behavior, "Do unto others as you
would have them do unto you." There are, however, other cultures with different standards for fairness in negotiations. It is a
good idea to consider whether you are behaving in a way you
would consider fair if you were on the receiving end.

When you consider the issue of fairness as one of the Seven
Pillars of Negotiational Wisdom, recognize that the perception of
your behavior and the fairness of the process can determine
whether other negotiating parties will feel comfortable with
and committed to the
result. If your priority is to
reach an agreement, the
perceived fairness of the
process may be your
greatest concern.

Fairness has another
aspect to it: Think about its
impact on your reputation
as a negotiator and as a
person. People don't want
to do business with folks who are likely to treat them unfairly.
Remember the old saying, "Cheat me once, shame on you.
Cheat me twice, shame on me."

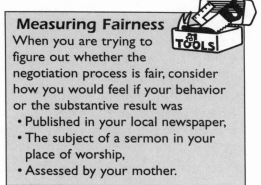

Measuring Fairness
When you are trying to
figure out whether the
negotiation process is fair, consider
how you would feel if your behavior
or the substantive result was
• Published in your local newspaper,
• The subject of a sermon in your
  place of worship,
• Assessed by your mother.

Market and Cultural Standards

Your preparation should include careful review of the standards of
behavior practiced in the market or culture where you are negotiating. While there are many exceptions to the generalities that
people apply to the fairness of used car dealers, people from different countries, or folks with other characteristics, a sense of

The Rug Merchant

A Bostonian traveling in Central Asia in the 1980s saw a carpet he wanted in a native market. The first element he negotiated with the rug merchant was the currency to be used in the transaction. They agreed to use German marks. Once the deal was complete, the Bostonian paid not in West German marks, a valued currency, but in East German marks, a currency that could not be converted and that had no value. When the tourist returned home, he invited a group of friends to view his carpet. They admired his choice—until he told them how he'd paid with valueless currency. At that point, his friends told him they were disgusted with his behavior and that his reputation was ruined. He had treated the merchant unfairly and his friends would not forget his inappropriate dealings.

appropriate behavior in a particular business or culture can prevent you from making mistakes. While you don't want to be unfair, you should be aware of what is generally considered normal in the situation. Do your homework, then open your mind to the possibility of exceptions to the generally accepted rules.

Grumpiness Factor

You negotiate in order to bring additional resources to serve your interests. Reaching a deal using an unfair approach means that the resources you are hoping to gain from other parties may not be made available. If people feel treated unfairly, they are less likely to fulfill their side of the bargain. Whether you are faced with issues of fairness based on culture or market or within a familiar setting, your counterparts' feelings about how fairly they have been treated will influence their willingness to fulfill their part of the bargain.

Commitment

A negotiation can only be called successful when it yields an agreement to which the parties are committed. When you analyze the negotiation process after negotiations are over, pay close attention to what you have learned about the likelihood that the parties will fulfill their part of the agreement. Look for benchmarks or other measures that reflect the likelihood that your counterparts will do what they promise.

Confidence Building and Benchmarking

Don't wait until after the agreement is reached to develop a sense of the dependability of the other parties. There are some things you can watch for in the negotiation process that may raise—or lower—your expectations about the other parties' commitment to fulfill their obligations:

- Have they been consistent or have they changed their story in their attempts to influence you?
- Have they lied about any of the issues?
- How have they demonstrated their authority to make decisions on behalf of their company?
- Did they treat you with respect?
- Were pre-negotiation agreements about agenda items implemented, or did they try to avoid issues important to you or sneak in issues about which you weren't prepared?
- If their reputation is less than perfect, what kind of guarantees have they given you of their future performance?

Monitoring Fulfillment

Think like a lawyer when you negotiate. Always ask yourself, "What's the worst that can happen?" Taking this cautious view should help you craft an agreement that includes appropriate fail-safe mechanisms should a party's commitment appear to flag during the implementation of the agreement. You can include incentives or penalties in the agreement to assure timely performance or fulfillment of specifications. Or you can include a list of resources that will be devoted to implementing the deal. If you do decide to build these elements into the agreement, they must become an integral part of the negotiation. Trying to add them afterward is too late. Comprehending the relative importance of achieving commitment as a consequence of your negotiations can help you protect yourself from making unwise agreements.

Part of the problem in monitoring fulfillment is the question of whether each side should be the judge of its own performance. This might lead to a situation of your word against theirs. In those circumstances, a perfectly acceptable agreement may fall apart. You and the other negotiators need to determine whether an objective disinterested third party should be named in the agreement as the mechanism for resolving disputes. Some major corporations follow the practices recommended by the CPR Institute of Dispute Resolution in New York City: In their contracts, the companies include standard clauses developed by CPR requiring mediation and/or arbitration before litigation over disagreements.

Communication

The enduring lesson about communication is to remember that God gave us two ears and one mouth and that we should use them in that ratio. If you look at communication as one of the Seven Pillars, you may recall that information is the fundamental asset in negotiation—and communication is how information moves from one party to others. Your Interest Map will tell you what information you need to reach a wise, durable agreement; it outlines the questions you need to ask to validate assumptions and learn about other parties' interests.

Communication Keys

As you assess the role communication plays in your negotiation, keep the following issues in mind:

- Communication is a two-way street; you need a presenter of information and an audience.
- The information you exchange informs you of changes in your BATNA as well as the BATNAs of other parties.
- Overcome the instinct to think of what you're going to say when another party is finished; focus on what they are revealing about themselves.
- You can't reach a wise agreement unless the parties understand each other and share an understanding of the agreement's details. Proper communication brings clarity to the process.
- Your communication style demonstrates whether you respect other parties and may even give them a sense of your commitment to fulfill the agreement.
- The best way to gain information is to ask questions and listen carefully to the answers.

Transparency

Communicating successfully brings transparency to the negotiation process. Transparency builds trust. With a transparent communication process, the negotiators are not trying to pull a fast one on each other. They are demonstrating that the negotiation process is fair. Using clear communication methods reduces the likelihood of surprise during the negotiation as well as during the lifetime of the resulting agreement. It is no less important to remember that you must communicate your concerns clearly; diplomatic assertiveness can protect you from being treated like a country bumpkin.

Foundation of the Seven Pillars

While the importance of each of the Seven Pillars may vary from negotiation to negotiation, it is crucial to remember that the Seven Pillars are supported by one foundation: PREPARATION. When you have time to prepare, you will be more confident and more competent in your negotiations. If you prepare regularly, you develop instincts that will enhance your effectiveness even when you don't have a chance to prepare.

Using an Interest Map as your preparation tool will enhance the mental discipline you bring to the negotiation process. While there may be other mechanisms that work for you, your preparation will work best if your process is consistent in its structure. Keeping the stakeholders and their interests at the forefront of your planning will enhance your comfort with the negotiation process. In this way, you will come to view negotiation not as a chore but simply as a means of communicating and col-

> **Follow the Guide's Advice**
>
> A young woman was visiting New York City. As part of her sightseeing, she wanted to visit Carnegie Hall. When she asked a New Yorker, "How can I get to Carnegie Hall?" he responded by looking closely at her and saying, "Practice. Practice. Practice." The more you practice your negotiation skills, the stronger they will become.

laborating with others in order to create agreements that respond to your interests and to those of your constituencies.

Manager's Checklist for Chapter 12

❑ You need to prioritize among seven elements of the negotiation process, called The Seven Pillars of Negotiational Wisdom. Their relative importance varies with each negotiation:
  • Relationship
  • Interests
  • BATNA
  • Creativity
  • Fairness
  • Commitment
  • Communication

❑ Since most people tend to negotiate with the same parties time after time, it is wise to view each negotiation as an episode in an ongoing relationship.

❑ Successful external negotiations depend on successful internal negotiations—within your company, your division, or even your family.

❑ Remember that negotiation is not a competitive sport. You will have more long-run success if you focus on your interests rather than combat with your negotiation counterparts.

❑ The reason you are negotiating is because you don't have all the answers; other parties' contributions can add value to how your interests are served by the agreement.

❑ Pay attention to your walking-in BATNA as you prepare for negotiation. Watch how that BATNA may change as information is brought forward during the negotiation process.

❑ Increasing the number of bargaining chips by using creative thinking can add value to the agreement. Don't forget to compare negotiation with weaving; the contributions of multiple parties can yield a more durable agreement than one based entirely on a single party's input.

❑ Unless the parties feel fairly treated in the negotiation process, they may not buy in and feel ownership of the agreement.

❑ Do a good job of learning about fairness etiquette in the business sectors or marketplaces in which you are dealing. How you behave can determine the outcome at least as much as the substantive elements of the deal you offer.

❑ Approach every negotiation with an eye on the long-term results you seek. Build incentives for performance into the agreement. Develop benchmarks that will give you early warning of risk if the agreement—or its fulfillment—may be in jeopardy.

❑ The communication that is most effective in negotiation involves using your ears, not your mouth. Paying attention to other parties not only shows respect, it can also yield information crucial to your decision making.

❑ Preparation is fundamental to success in negotiation. Using preparation tools such as the Interest Map whenever you have the opportunity will not only improve the negotiations for which you have prepared. The practice will also enhance the negotiation instincts you use when you have not had a chance to prepare.

Index